VEGETABLE

RECIPES AND TEXT
MARLENA SPIELER

GENERAL EDITOR
CHUCK WILLIAMS

PHOTOGRAPHS
MAREN CARUSO

APPLE

CONTENTS

THE CLASSICS

SPRING

SUMMER

AUTUMN

WINTER

MAIN DISHES

INTRODUCTION

With the recent explosion of farmers' markets across the country, there is no longer any need to settle for less when it comes to shopping for vegetables. Those red tomatoes and bell peppers on the supermarket shelves may look pretty, but if the ripeness and flavor are not truly there, just pass them by. If you search out locally grown vegetables at their seasonal peak—or grow them in your own garden—you will be richly rewarded at the table. And the sheer variety of vegetables in the markets is unrivaled.

Thumb through the pages of this book to find recipes that make the most of each season's offerings and capture each season's mood. Alongside each recipe, an informative side note highlights a particular technique or ingredient, deepening your knowledge of cooking, while the last chapter covers all the basics of vegetable cookery. I hope that this book inspires you to prepare fresh and healthful meals using all the wonderful types of vegetables that are available to us today.

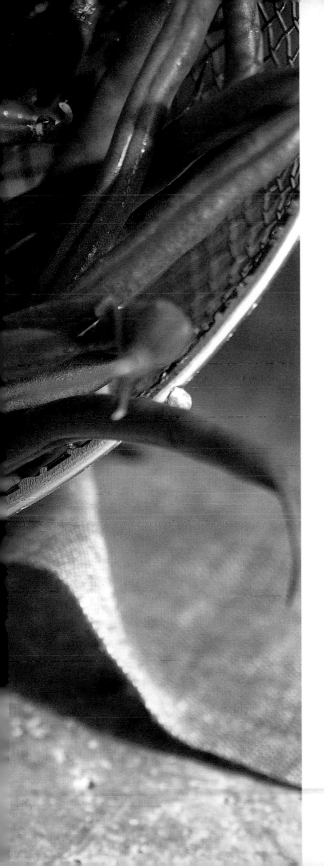

THE CLASSICS

These timeless vegetable recipes have earned their status as classics for two reasons: simplicity and versatility. From spring peas with fresh mint to creamy mashed potatoes, assembly is straightforward, and each dish complements a variety of menus, from a weeknight family supper to a holiday meal.

GLAZED CARROTS

Cut the carrots into large julienne about 3 inches (7.5 cm) long and ¼ inch (6 mm) wide and thick *(left)*.

In a large, deep, heavy frying pan, melt the butter over medium heat. Add the carrots and sugar, ginger, salt, and pepper to taste. Stir together and cook for 1–2 minutes. Add water to just cover the carrots, raise the heat to high, cover, and cook until the water boils and the carrots turn bright orange, about 5 minutes. (Do not add too much water, as it will take longer to evaporate and the carrots will become mushy.)

Uncover and continue to cook the carrots over medium-high heat until the water evaporates, 5–7 minutes longer. Continue to cook for a few minutes longer, allowing the carrots to caramelize a bit in the butter-sugar mixture. Garnish with the parsley, if using, and serve at once.

Variation Tip: Other vegetables—turnips, parsnips, rutabagas, onions—can be julienned and glazed in the same way, adjusting the cooking time as necessary.

MAKES 4 SERVINGS

1½–2 lb (750 g–1 kg) carrots, peeled

3–4 tablespoons (1½–2 oz/ 45–60 g) unsalted butter

2–3 tablespoons sugar

⅛ teaspoon ground ginger, or to taste

Salt and freshly ground pepper

1 tablespoon chopped fresh flat-leaf (Italian) parsley (optional)

JULIENNING

When a recipe calls for a julienne, also known as matchsticks, use a chef's knife or mandoline (page 114) to cut the vegetable, meat, cheese, or other food into long, narrow, thin strips. Many recipes indicate what size the strips should be. For those that don't, the strips are typically 2 inches (5 cm) long and ⅛ inch (3 mm) wide and thick. To julienne any food, first cut it into pieces the length of the desired julienne.

Then cut each piece lengthwise into slices as thick as the desired julienne. Finally, stack the slices and again cut them lengthwise, into narrow strips.

FRESH PEAS WITH MINT

16 pearl onions

4 tablespoons (2 oz/60 g) unsalted butter

Salt and freshly ground pepper

1 teaspoon sugar

2 lb (1 kg) English peas, shelled (about 2 cups/ 10 oz/315 g)

1 small head butter (Boston) lettuce, leaves separated and coarsely chopped

1 tablespoon chopped fresh flat-leaf (Italian) parsley

1 tablespoon chopped fresh mint or pinch of dried mint, crumbled (see Note)

Bring a saucepan three-fourths full of water to a boil, add the pearl onions, and blanch for 1 minute. Drain and immerse in cold water for 5 minutes to stop the cooking. Drain again and slip off the skins; they should come off easily. Using a paring knife, trim away the root and stem ends.

In a heavy saucepan, melt half of the butter over medium-low heat. Add the pearl onions and sauté until they are pale gold in spots and have softened slightly, about 8 minutes. Sprinkle them with salt and pepper and about half of the sugar and mix well.

Add the peas, lettuce, parsley, mint, and the remaining sugar. Stir well and season to taste with salt and pepper. Pour water into the pan to just cover the peas. Raise the heat to medium-high, bring the mixture to a boil, reduce the heat to very low, cover, and simmer gently until the peas are tender, 5–8 minutes.

Drain and place in a warmed serving bowl. Add the remaining butter, toss to melt and coat evenly, and serve at once.

Note: For this dish, use spearmint rather than peppermint, as the latter is too strongly flavored. Instead of the mint, you can also use 1–2 tablespoons chopped fresh basil or additional flat-leaf (Italian) parsley or 1 teaspoon each chopped fresh thyme and marjoram or summer savory.

MAKES 4 SERVINGS

SHELLING PEAS

To shell peas, hold a pod over a large bowl, squeeze the pod slightly to split it open, and then run your thumbnail down along the seam to pop out the peas, capturing them in the bowl. Shell peas just before cooking to prevent them from drying out. If fresh peas are not in the market, frozen petite peas serve as a good substitute and will cook in the same amount of time as young peas.

MASHED POTATOES

MASHED POTATO SAVVY

There's more than one way to cook—and mash—a potato. In this recipe, the potatoes are cooked whole with the peel on to keep them from becoming waterlogged, then peeled before mashing. Some prefer mashed potatoes with lumps, others like them perfectly smooth. For lumps, mash them with a potato masher. For a silky smooth texture, use a ricer or an electric mixer, or start with a masher and finish them off with a sturdy whisk. Never use a food processor, as its powerful action will give the potatoes a gummy texture.

Put the unpeeled whole potatoes in a large saucepan with water to cover by about 2 inches (5 cm). Add large pinches of salt and sugar. (The sugar brings out the natural flavor of the potatoes yet does not contribute any sweetness to the final dish.) Bring the potatoes to a boil over high heat. Reduce the heat to medium and cook, covered, until the potatoes are tender, 25–35 minutes, depending on size. Test with a fork; the potatoes should pierce easily. (Do not boil the potatoes until they are falling apart, as they will be difficult to drain and your mashed potatoes will be watery.)

Drain the potatoes and, when cool enough to handle, peel them. Return the peeled potatoes to the pan over low heat and, shaking the pan, dry the potatoes briefly. Remove from the heat. Using a potato masher or an electric mixer, mash the potatoes *(left)*. Alternatively, pass the peeled potatoes through a ricer held over the pan.

Return the pan to low heat and add the butter, working it in with a spoon or whisk. Stir in ¼ cup hot milk plus more as needed and salt and pepper to taste. Serve immediately or try any of the following variations.

Garlic Mashed Potatoes: Add 1 or 2 cloves garlic, sliced, to the milk as you heat it, then strain out the garlic before using the milk.

Pesto Mashed Potatoes: Reduce the amount of milk to 2–3 tablespoons, then beat in ¼–½ cup (2–4 fl oz/60–125 ml) pesto (page 111), or to taste.

Roquefort Mashed Potatoes: Add ¼ lb (125 g) Roquefort cheese, crumbled; 1 clove garlic, minced; and a squeeze of lemon juice to the potatoes as you mash them. Serve sprinkled with chopped fresh parsley or chives.

MAKES 4 SERVINGS

4 or 5 large russet potatoes or Yukon gold potatoes, about 2–2½ lb (1–1.25 kg) total weight

Salt and freshly ground pepper

Pinch of sugar

4 tablespoons (2 oz/60 g) unsalted butter, or to taste

¼–½ cup (2–4 fl oz/ 60–125 ml) milk, heavy (double) cream, or half-and-half (half cream), heated

SPINACH SAUTÉED WITH RAISINS AND PINE NUTS

Put the raisins in a small heatproof bowl and add boiling water to cover. Cover the bowl and leave to plump for about 10 minutes. Drain and set aside.

Meanwhile, if desired, toast the pine nuts by heating them gently in a dry small, heavy frying pan over medium heat, tossing them every so often as they become golden and fragrant, 2–4 minutes. Watch the pine nuts closely, as they burn easily. When toasted, immediately pour onto a plate.

In a frying pan, heat the olive oil over medium heat. Add the onion and sauté lightly until golden, 5–8 minutes. Add the garlic and sauté for 1 minute longer. Remove the pan from the heat and set aside.

Put the spinach with just the rinsing water clinging to the leaves in a saucepan over medium-high heat, cover, and cook until the spinach is bright green and wilted, 1–2 minutes. Remove from the heat and drain well in a sieve, pressing the spinach with the back of a spoon to remove excess moisture. When the spinach is cool enough to handle, chop it coarsely. (If using baby spinach leaves, omit the chopping.)

Add the spinach, drained raisins, and pine nuts to the onion and garlic in the frying pan and return to medium heat. Stir until the spinach and onion are heated through, 1–2 minutes. Season to taste with salt and pepper. Serve hot or at room temperature.

Variation Tips: Use golden raisins (sultanas) or large muscatel raisins in place of the black raisins, and slivered blanched almonds in place of the pine nuts.

MAKES 4 SERVINGS

¼ cup (1½ oz/45 g) raisins

¼ cup (1¼ oz/37 g) pine nuts

2 tablespoons extra-virgin olive oil

1 yellow onion, finely chopped

1 clove garlic, chopped

2 lb (1 kg) spinach leaves, tough stems removed and leaves well rinsed

Salt and freshly ground black pepper or cayenne pepper

PINE NUTS

Look for shelled pine nuts that are long and oval rather than stubby and round. The former, which are primarily European-grown nuts, have a delicate flavor, while the latter, which are Asian in origin, have a sharper flavor. Purchase pine nuts from markets with a good turnover, as they have a short shelf life due to their naturally high concentration of oil. Store the nuts in an airtight container in a cool place away from light for shorter periods, or in the refrigerator or freezer for longer periods.

BROCCOLI WITH HOLLANDAISE SAUCE

FOR THE HOLLANDAISE SAUCE:

2 egg yolks

Pinch of salt

Small pinch of cayenne pepper

Juice of ½ lemon (about 1½ tablespoons), or to taste

2 tablespoons chilled unsalted butter, cut into small pieces

½ cup (4 oz/125 g) unsalted butter, melted and kept warm

Pinch of salt

Pinch of sugar

1 large or 2 small to medium broccoli stalks (see Notes), about 2 lb (1 kg) total weight, trimmed into florets and bite-sized pieces

To make the hollandaise sauce, in the top pan of a double boiler *(right)*, whisk the egg yolks until they are blended and foamy. Stir in the salt, cayenne pepper, 1 tablespoon of the lemon juice, and half of the chilled butter pieces. Set the top pan over, but not touching, simmering water in the bottom pan and reduce the heat to low. Continue to whisk until the eggs thicken slightly and the butter melts, about 5 minutes. If the mixture seems in danger of thickening too fast and curdling, remove the top pan from the heat and continue beating, adding a little more chilled butter if needed.

Begin adding the melted butter, a few drops at a time, beating after each addition until it is fully absorbed. Once the mixture has emulsified and thickened, start adding the butter a little more quickly, first 1 teaspoon at a time and then 1 tablespoon at a time, beating well after each addition.

Remove the top pan from the heat and whisk in the remaining chilled butter. Taste and add the remaining lemon juice, if needed. Taste again and adjust the seasoning with salt and cayenne pepper. The sauce can be kept warm for up to 30 minutes by placing the top pan over hot (but not simmering) water in the bottom pan. Whisk the sauce occasionally to keep it from separating.

Bring a saucepan three-fourths full of water to a boil. Add large pinches of salt and sugar and the broccoli and boil until the broccoli is bright green and tender-crisp, 1–2 minutes. Drain well.

Serve the broccoli topped with the hollandaise sauce.

Notes: Hollandaise sauce contains egg that may be only partially cooked; for more information, see page 113. If the broccoli stalks seem tough, peel them with a vegetable peeler or paring knife before trimming.

MAKES 4 SERVINGS

DOUBLE BOILERS

A specialized pan used for gentle cooking, a double boiler consists of one pan nested atop another with room for water to simmer in the lower pan. The top pan should not touch the water in the lower pan, and the water should never boil. A tight fit between the pans ensures that no water or steam mixes with the ingredients. If you don't have a double boiler, choose a heatproof bowl that fits snugly on top of a saucepan and nest the two together.

GRATIN DAUPHINOISE

Cut the potatoes crosswise into slices ⅛ inch (3 mm) thick. You can do it by hand with a sharp knife or with a mandoline, or, for less tidy slices, in a food processor. Place the sliced potatoes in a large bowl, add cold water to cover, and let them soak for at least 15 minutes and up to 1 hour.

Position a rack in the upper third of the oven and preheat to 325°F (165°C). Place a baking sheet on the rack below to catch any drips. Rub the bottom and sides of a 2-qt (2-l) wide, shallow baking dish with the cut sides of the halved garlic clove, if using. Then grease the dish with the 2 tablespoons room-temperature butter.

Drain the potato slices and dry well with a kitchen towel. Cut the 4 tablespoons butter into small pieces. Arrange a layer of the potato slices in the prepared baking dish, sprinkle with salt and pepper, dot with pieces of the butter, and add a light scattering of chopped garlic, if using. Repeat the layering until all the potatoes are used, finishing with potatoes and reserving some of the butter for the top of the gratin. The potatoes should reach no higher than to within ½ inch (12 mm) of the rim of the dish. Pour the cream evenly over the potatoes. Dot bits of butter across the top of the potatoes and sprinkle with salt and pepper.

Cover the gratin with aluminum foil and bake until the potatoes are translucent and the cream is bubbling, 30–40 minutes. Uncover and bake until the top is crusty and the potatoes are completely tender when pierced with a knife, about 30 minutes longer. If the gratin seems dry, baste the top occasionally with the liquid in the dish. Serve the gratin at once, directly from the dish.

Serving Tip: After baking, sprinkle the gratin with chopped fresh parsley and pink peppercorns for a colorful, confetti-like garnish.

MAKES 4 SERVINGS

A CLASSIC GRATIN

This potato gratin hails from the Dauphine region of eastern France. It is easy to make, but some special touches are necessary. First, the sliced potatoes must be rinsed or soaked and then dried well, to remove excess starch that would make the dish gummy. Salt should be added with a generous hand, and plenty of butter and cream should be poured in to achieve a silky, unctuous quality. Cheese is not necessary, as the flavor of the crusty potatoes should dominate. If possible, choose a rustic ceramic baking dish that reflects this recipe's homey character.

5 large russet potatoes, about 2½ lb (1.25 kg) total weight, peeled

3–5 cloves garlic, chopped, plus 1 clove, halved (optional)

4 tablespoons (2 oz/60 g) unsalted butter, plus 2 tablespoons at room temperature

Salt and freshly ground pepper

1½ cups (12 fl oz/375 ml) heavy (double) cream

SPRING

Spring arrives in a wash of green: bundles of asparagus spears and mounds of English and sugar snap peas, sturdy artichokes and slender young onions. But the variety doesn't end there. For pretty touches of color at the dinner table, cooks turn to the season's small red, white, and yellow new potatoes; crisp radishes in reds, purples, and pastels; and tawny brown mushrooms.

MIXED SPRING MUSHROOMS WITH GARLIC BUTTER AND PINE NUTS

Preheat the oven to 450°F (230°C). Remove any of the tougher stems from the mushrooms and reserve for making soup or stock. Cut the larger mushrooms into pieces so that all the mushrooms, whole and cut, are about the same size. Arrange the mushrooms in a single layer in a large roasting pan.

In a bowl, using a spoon or whisk, mix together the butter to taste, garlic to taste, and salt and pepper to taste. Spread it on the tops of the mushrooms, or dot the tops with small dollops. Sprinkle the wine evenly over all.

Roast the mushrooms until they begin to sizzle and brown, about 15 minutes. Remove from the oven, sprinkle with the pine nuts, and return to the oven to continue roasting until the mushrooms are cooked through and browned in places, about 10 minutes longer. The total amount of roasting time depends on the types of mushrooms used; certain varieties will take longer than others to cook. Taste and adjust the seasoning.

Transfer to a warm serving dish and sprinkle with the chives. Serve at once.

Variation Tip: Slivered blanched almonds can be used in place of the pine nuts in this recipe. Toast and use as you would the pine nuts.

MAKES 4 SERVINGS

WILD MUSHROOMS
One often sees the term *wild mushrooms* in recipes, on menus, and elsewhere, but *exotic mushrooms* is generally a more accurate description, as most wild mushrooms we eat today are, in fact, cultivated. Among those not cultivated to date are musky-flavored morels, a springtime favorite, and autumn's chanterelles, porcini (cèpes), matsutakes, and black trumpets. Such wonderful varieties as oysters, shiitakes, portobellos, and cremini are all successfully farmed.

1 lb (500 g) mixed large fresh spring mushrooms such as morel, portobello, shiitake, oyster, cremini, and white button, brushed clean

4–6 tablespoons (2–4 oz/ 60–125 g) unsalted butter, at room temperature

3–5 cloves garlic, chopped

Salt and freshly ground pepper

2 tablespoons dry white wine

⅓ cup (2 oz/60 g) pine nuts

1–2 tablespoons chopped fresh chives or flat-leaf (Italian) parsley

ROASTED ASPARAGUS FOUR WAYS

2 bunches (2 lb/1 kg) asparagus, preferably thick, trimmed, and peeled if needed *(far right)*

2 tablespoons dry white wine or dry vermouth

Salt and freshly ground pepper

3 tablespoons extra-virgin olive oil

Juice of ½ lemon

Position a rack in the upper third of the oven and preheat to 450°F (230°C). In a large, shallow baking pan, toss together the asparagus, wine, salt and pepper to taste, and olive oil until the asparagus spears are evenly coated.

Roast the asparagus until the the spears are browned in spots and are just tender-crisp, about 10 minutes. Do not overcook.

Transfer the asparagus to a platter and drizzle with the lemon juice to taste. Serve at once or try any of the following variations.

Roasted Asparagus with Shaved Parmesan: Drizzle the hot roasted asparagus with lemon juice as directed, then, using a cheese shaver, a vegetable peeler, or a paring knife, shave 1–2 oz (30–60 g) Parmesan, pecorino romano, Asiago, or dry Jack cheese over the asparagus.

Roasted Asparagus with Pesto: Omit the lemon juice. Toss the hot roasted asparagus with 1–2 tablespoons pesto (page 111), or to taste. Serve at once.

Roasted Asparagus with Hollandaise: Drizzle the hot roasted asparagus with lemon juice as directed, then serve it with hollandaise sauce (page 21).

MAKES 4 SERVINGS

TRIMMING ASPARAGUS

When preparing asparagus for cooking, check for a tough, fibrous inedible portion at the base of each spear. You can cut off the dry, coarse-looking base or simply break off the tough end of each spear by bending it gently until it snaps. It will break precisely where the tender part ends and the tough part begins. If the skin seems thick and tough, use a vegetable peeler or paring knife to peel the stalk to within about 2 inches (5 cm) of the tip. This will help the asparagus cook more evenly.

FAVA BEANS WITH SERRANO HAM AND FRIED EGG

In a large frying pan, heat 2 tablespoons of the olive oil over medium heat. Add the onion, garlic, and ham and cook until the onion is softened, about 5 minutes. Add the peeled favas and stir for a moment, taking care not to break them up, then add the sherry, stock, and parsley. Cook over high heat until the liquid reduces a bit and the flavors are blended, about 1 minute. Add another tablespoon of the olive oil, season to taste with salt and pepper, and transfer to a serving bowl. Keep warm.

In the same pan, heat the remaining 1 tablespoon oil. Crack the egg into the pan and fry until the yolk is still runny but the white is firm, about 2 minutes. A little bit of crispy edge to the white is fine and adds good texture.

To serve, cut the egg into bite-sized pieces and toss with the warm fava mixture. The runny yolk melds into the sauce. Serve sprinkled with the chives.

Note: Similar to Italian prosciutto, serrano ham is Spanish in origin. Both are made by salting a leg of pork and hanging it to air-cure. Traditionally cut thicker than prosciutto, serrano has a similar but more earthy flavor. It can be found in delicatessens and specialty-food stores.

MAKES 4 SERVINGS

SKINNING FAVA BEANS

Fresh fava beans must be removed from their pods before cooking. Unless the beans are very small and young, the tough skin that covers each bean must also be slipped off. To remove the skins, blanch the shelled beans in rapidly boiling salted water until just tender, 1–2 minutes. Do not overcook. Drain and rinse under cold running water. Pinch each bean opposite the end where it was attached to the pod and squeeze; the bean should pop free. Use a paring knife to remove any stubborn skins.

4 tablespoons (2 fl oz/ 60 ml) extra-virgin olive oil

1 yellow onion or 3 shallots, finely chopped

2 cloves garlic, chopped

3 oz (90 g) sliced serrano ham (see Note) or prosciutto, cut into thin strips

1–1½ lb (500–750 g) young fava (broad) beans, shelled and skinned *(far left)*

½ cup (4 fl oz/125 ml) dry sherry

½ cup (4 fl oz/125 ml) chicken or vegetable stock or low-sodium canned broth

1 tablespoon chopped fresh flat-leaf (Italian) parsley

Salt and freshly ground pepper

1 egg

1 tablespoon chopped chives

NEW POTATOES WITH SPRING PEAS

2 lb (1 kg) small new potatoes such as fingerlings or red or white potatoes, of uniform size

Salt and freshly ground pepper

Pinch of sugar

2 cups (10 oz/315 g) shelled young English peas

2 tablespoons unsalted butter

2 tablespoons extra-virgin olive oil

5 or 6 green (spring) onions, white and tender green parts, thinly sliced

Put the potatoes in a large saucepan with enough water to cover by 2 inches (5 cm). Add large pinches of salt and sugar. (The sugar brings out the natural flavor of the potatoes yet does not contribute any sweetness to the final dish.) Bring the potatoes to a boil over high heat. Reduce the heat to medium and cook at a bubbling simmer, uncovered, until the potatoes are just tender, 15–20 minutes. Test with a fork; the fork should meet a bit of resistance, but pierce the potatoes easily. (Do not let the potatoes overcook, or they will become watery and fall apart.)

Drain the potatoes. They may be peeled or left unpeeled. If you are peeling them, rinse them in cold water and leave to cool for a few minutes, then peel.

Meanwhile, bring a saucepan three-fourths full of water to a rapid boil. Add pinches of salt and sugar and the peas, and blanch until they turn bright green, about 30 seconds. Drain and rinse under cold running water to stop the cooking and set the color.

In a heavy frying pan, melt the butter with the olive oil over medium-low heat. Add the green onions and let them wilt, about 3 minutes. Add the potatoes and peas and toss together until heated through, about 5 minutes. Season to taste with salt and pepper and serve at once.

Variation Tip: Try substituting 2 cups (9½ oz/300 g) sugar snap peas or 2 cups (6½ oz/200 g) trimmed snow peas (mangetouts) for the English peas in this recipe if desired.

MAKES 4 SERVINGS

NEW POTATOES

New potatoes, the first potatoes dug in spring and early summer, taste earthy and satisfying but nothing like the heftier mature potatoes found in markets the rest of the year. These young potatoes are low in starch, with thin, tender skins and delicate flesh. Small round red or white potatoes (also called creamers), fingerlings, and Yellow Finns are among the most common varieties available as new potatoes. Unlike mature potatoes, new potatoes should be stored no more than 2 or 3 days before cooking and eating.

ARTICHOKE HEARTS IN LEMON-PARSLEY SAUCE

If using fresh whole artichokes, trim away the tough outer leaves and remove the choke *(left)*. Bring a large saucepan three-fourths full of water to a boil. Drain the artichokes, add them to the boiling water along with the lemon half, and parboil for 5 minutes. Drain and set aside. (There is no need to parboil frozen artichoke hearts.)

If using salt-packed capers, soak in water to cover for 5 minutes, then drain and pat dry. If using brine-packed capers, rinse under cold running water, then drain and pat dry. Set the artichokes and capers aside.

In a sauté pan or deep frying pan, heat 2 tablespoons of the olive oil over medium-low heat. Add the onions and sauté lightly until softened and golden, 5–6 minutes. Add the garlic, parsley, and artichokes, and cook, tossing every so often and adding a little more oil if the artichokes begin to scorch, until they are fragrant and lightly golden, about 10 minutes. Season the artichokes to taste with salt and pepper.

Add 2 more tablespoons olive oil, 1 cup of the stock, the capers, the lemon zest (if using), the lemon juice, and the basil. Raise the heat to high and bring to a boil. Reduce the heat to medium and cook, uncovered, until the artichokes are tender and the liquid has evaporated to a thickened and flavorful sauce, about 20 minutes. If the liquid is in danger of boiling away before the artichokes are tender, add more stock as needed.

Transfer to a serving bowl and serve hot or at room temperature.

MAKES 4 SERVINGS

TRIMMING ARTICHOKES

Working with 1 artichoke at a time, snap off the tough outer leaves until you reach the pale green inner leaves. Cut off the stem and trim off the thorny leaf tops with a serrated knife. If using small artichokes, gently spread the leaves and, with a paring knife or small spoon, cut or scoop out the fuzzy choke. If using medium-sized artichokes, quarter them lengthwise and cut out the chokes. Drop into a large bowl of cold water to which you have added the juice of 1 lemon to prevent discoloration while you trim the remaining artichokes.

8 small to medium artichokes, trimmed *(far left),* or 15–20 thawed frozen artichoke hearts

½ lemon

1 tablespoon capers, preferably salt packed (optional)

4–5 tablespoons (2–2½ fl oz/ 60–75 ml) extra-virgin olive oil

2 yellow onions, finely chopped

4–5 cloves garlic, coarsely chopped

3 tablespoons chopped fresh flat-leaf (Italian) parsley

Salt and freshly ground pepper

1–2 cups (8–16 fl oz/ 250–500 ml) vegetable or chicken stock or low-sodium canned broth

½ teaspoon grated lemon zest (optional)

Juice of 1 lemon

A few fresh basil or mint leaves, torn

SUMMER

The summertime farmers' market is a visual feast. Vine-ripe tomatoes in reds, golds, and purples draw shoppers toward one stand, while bright summer squashes in shades of yellow and green beckon from another. Such ingredients, along with a bounty of peppers and eggplants, can be used in simple, quick preparations that leave time for enjoying long, sunny days.

GRILLED CORN WITH CHILE-LIME BUTTER

CHOOSING CORN

When shopping for corn on the cob, select ears that have pale yellow silk and evenly green husks with no signs of brown. The kernels should be packed tightly without dry spaces in between, and they should be plump, moist, and fairly evenly spaced. When corn is fresh from the garden and very sweet, it can be eaten raw. But most corn needs to be cooked briefly—and as soon after harvest as possible—to bring out its best flavor. It can be steamed or boiled, but is particularly good when cooked on the grill.

In a bowl, using a wooden spoon, mix together the butter and garlic until well blended. Work in the chile powder, paprika, cumin, and cilantro until well mixed. Season to taste with salt and pepper, then squeeze in the lime juice and mix again. Cover and refrigerate for at least 30 minutes to blend the flavors, then let sit at room temperature for about 30 minutes before serving. If the lime juice separates out upon standing, stir to reblend.

Prepare a fire in a charcoal or gas grill. Meanwhile, in a small bowl, using a fork, work together the olive oil and 1 tablespoon of the chile-lime butter until well blended. Spread or brush the mixture lightly onto the corn.

Grill the ears of corn, turning as needed, until evenly cooked through and lightly charred in places and golden in others but not heavily scorched, 5–6 minutes. The kernels should taste tender and sweet but also have the scent of the fire.

Transfer to a platter and serve at once with the remaining chile-lime butter and salt and pepper.

Note: Chile-lime butter is also delicious on grilled or fire-roasted sweet potatoes or yams. Or, spread it onto bread, garlic-bread style, and heat the bread over a charcoal fire.

Serving Tip: Allow for 2 ears of corn per person if this is your only side dish, if the ears are on the small side, or if you are serving devoted corn-on-the-cob eaters.

MAKES 4–6 SERVINGS

FOR THE CHILE-LIME BUTTER:

½ cup (4 oz/125 g) unsalted butter, at room temperature

3 cloves garlic, minced

½–1 teaspoon mild chile powder, preferably New Mexican, or to taste

Large pinch of paprika

Large pinch of ground cumin

2–3 tablespoons chopped fresh cilantro (fresh coriander)

Salt and freshly ground pepper

Juice of ¼–½ lime

1 tablespoon olive oil

4–8 ears of corn, husks and silk removed

Salt and freshly ground pepper

HEIRLOOM TOMATO SALAD

6–8 very ripe heirloom tomatoes, in a variety of sizes, shapes, and colors

¼–½ teaspoon sugar

Salt

2 green (spring) onions, ¼ red onion, or 1 shallot, chopped

2 cloves garlic, finely chopped (optional)

2 teaspoons minced fresh oregano, or to taste

Balsamic vinegar

Sherry vinegar or white wine vinegar

3–5 tablespoons (1½–2½ fl oz/45–75 ml) extra-virgin olive oil

Coarse country bread for serving

Slice the tomatoes, capturing their juices in a bowl. Layer the tomatoes on a platter, sprinkling them with the sugar, salt to taste, green onions, garlic (if using), oregano, and the captured juices as you arrange them.

Finish with a sprinkling each of balsamic vinegar and sherry vinegar to taste and then drizzle with olive oil to taste. Let stand until ready to serve, or for up to 2 hours.

Serve accompanied with the bread for sopping up the juices.

Variations: Other summery fresh herbs can be used in place of the oregano: 1 teaspoon chopped fresh thyme or rosemary, 1 tablespoon chopped fresh flat-leaf (Italian) parsley, or 2–3 tablespoons chopped fresh basil.

MAKES 4 SERVINGS

HEIRLOOM FRUITS AND VEGETABLES

Heirloom varieties are fruits and vegetables that were once cultivated but fell out of favor with big producers because they neither shipped nor stored well. Many of them have superior flavor, however, and small-scale farmers have reintroduced the best varieties to farmers' markets and greengrocers. Available in a wealth of sizes, flavors, and colors—yellow, orange, zebra striped—heirloom tomatoes are one of the glories of summer. Vendors at farmers' markets will often offer you a taste of each type before you make a final choice.

ESCALIVADA

Preheat the oven to 400°F (200°C). Cut the globe eggplant into 8 equal pieces or each of the Asian eggplants into 4 equal pieces. Quarter the bell peppers lengthwise and seed them. Combine the eggplant and bell pepper pieces in a roasting pan. Break the garlic heads into cloves. Reserve 2 cloves and add the others, unpeeled, to the pan with the vegetables. Trim the zucchini and cut each into 2 or 3 pieces. Cut off the stems and feathery tops and any bruised outer stalks from the fennel bulb and quarter it lengthwise. Add the zucchini, fennel, onions, and tomatoes to the pan. Sprinkle with sugar and season to taste with salt and pepper. Drizzle with the olive oil and vinegar. Mix all the ingredients together well.

Roast the vegetables, turning them once or even twice if they threaten to burn or cook unevenly, until tender, about 40 minutes. Avoid turning them too often, or they will collapse and become too saucy. You want them to keep their shape and character.

When the vegetables are tender, remove from the oven and transfer to a bowl. Peel and finely chop the reserved garlic cloves and sprinkle over the vegetables along with the parsley and rosemary. (To avoid breaking down the vegetables, do not stir the mixture at this point.) Serve hot or at room temperature, making sure that each diner receives some of each vegetable. The whole roasted garlic cloves may be squeezed and spread onto pieces of bread by each diner.

MAKES 4 SERVINGS

ESCALIVADA

A classic dish of Catalonia, in southeastern Spain, *escalivada* takes its name from the Spanish for "grilled," though it is often roasted, as in this version. Seasonal vegetables are cut into chunks, tossed into a rustic ceramic dish along with abundant olive oil, and then roasted. They emerge from the oven tender yet holding their shape. Serve the vegetables as an accompaniment to roasted meats or fish, toss with pasta, or simply eat with crusty bread. Leftovers are excellent and can be chopped up and scrambled with eggs or used to top a pizza.

1 globe eggplant (aubergine), trimmed, or 2 Asian (slender) eggplants, trimmed

3 bell peppers (capsicums), 1 *each* red, yellow, and green

2 heads garlic

4 zucchini (courgettes) or 2 zucchini and 2 yellow crookneck squashes

1 fennel bulb

2 red onions, quartered through stem end

3 or 4 tomatoes, halved crosswise

Sugar for sprinkling

Salt and freshly ground pepper

¼ cup (2 fl oz/60 ml) extra-virgin olive oil

Dash of sherry vinegar or red or white wine vinegar

2 tablespoons chopped fresh flat-leaf (Italian) parsley

1 teaspoon chopped fresh rosemary

Coarse country bread for serving

ZUCCHINI WITH ROASTED RED PEPPERS AND CHIVES

2 red bell peppers (capsicums)

2 cloves garlic, chopped (optional)

3–4 tablespoons chopped fresh chives

5–8 fresh basil leaves, thinly sliced

2 tablespoons extra-virgin olive oil

Balsamic vinegar

Salt and freshly ground pepper

Pinch of sugar (if boiling zucchini)

4 young, tender zucchini (courgettes), about 1 lb (500 g) total weight, diced or cut into bite-sized pieces

Preheat the broiler (grill). Put the bell peppers on a baking sheet and broil (grill), turning as needed, until blistered and charred on all sides, 10–15 minutes. Alternatively, using tongs or a large fork, hold the peppers, one at a time, over the flame of a gas burner and turn as needed until evenly blistered and charred. Transfer the blackened peppers to a brown paper bag and seal loosely, or to a covered bowl. Let cool to the touch. Remove the peppers and peel away the charred skin. Slit lengthwise and remove and discard the stems and seeds.

Finely chop the peppers and put in a serving bowl. Add the garlic, if using, chives and basil to taste, and the olive oil. Season to taste with vinegar, salt, and pepper. Set aside.

Bring a saucepan three-fourths full of water to a boil. Add pinches of salt and sugar and the zucchini and boil rapidly until the zucchini is tender-crisp, about 5 minutes. Drain the zucchini well. Alternatively, bring water to a boil in a steamer pan, put the zucchini in a steamer rack over the water, cover, and steam until tender-crisp, 3–4 minutes. Remove the zucchini from the rack.

Add the zucchini to the bell pepper mixture and toss well. Serve immediately.

MAKES 4 SERVINGS

BALSAMIC VINEGAR

True balsamic vinegar, made in the Italian region of Emilia-Romagna from white Trebbiano grapes, is aged in a series of barrels made of different woods for at least 12 years and sometimes much longer. Only then can it be designated *aceto balsamico tradizionale*. Because of its deep flavor, long-aged true balsamic vinegar is used sparingly as a condiment on finished dishes, as in this recipe. Lesser-aged true balsamic vinegars or high-quality supermarket balsamics are more widely available and are suitable for cooking.

SIMPLE SAUTÉED EGGPLANT

Put the eggplant in a large, shallow bowl and sprinkle with the cayenne and the black pepper to taste. If not already salted, season to taste with salt as well. Toss together to coat well.

Heat a large, heavy frying pan over medium heat. When it begins to smoke, add 3–4 tablespoons of the olive oil to the pan. Then add the eggplant and brown, stirring only once or twice and adding more olive oil as needed to prevent scorching. Too much stirring will cause the eggplant to become mushy. When the eggplant is almost tender and nicely browned, after about 15 minutes, add the shallots, garlic, and parsley. Toss together and cook until the shallots are tender, just a few minutes.

Taste and adjust the seasoning. Serve hot or at room temperature.

Serving Tips: Serve this eggplant as a side dish to roasted lamb. The sautéed eggplant cubes, crusty and brown on the outside yet tender within, can also transform a dish of simple spaghetti with tomato sauce into a Sicilian treat, pasta alla Norma. Simply scatter the cubes around the edge of the platter and serve.

Variation Tips: For a rustic Middle Eastern or Moroccan flavor, sprinkle about ½ teaspoon ground cumin over the browned eggplant at the end of cooking. Just before serving, toss in about ¼ cup (⅓ oz/10 g) chopped fresh cilantro (fresh coriander).

MAKES 4 SERVINGS

1 lb (500 g) eggplant (aubergine), cut into ¾-inch (2-cm) cubes, salted and drained if large (page 108)

Pinch of cayenne pepper

Salt and freshly ground black pepper

4–5 tablespoons (2–2½ fl oz/ 60–75 ml) extra-virgin olive oil, or as needed

4 shallots or 1 yellow onion, finely chopped

3–4 cloves garlic, chopped

3 tablespoons chopped fresh flat-leaf (Italian) parsley

EGGPLANT VARIETIES

The eggplant most cooks are familiar with is the globe eggplant, which is usually large, egg or pear shaped, with a thin, shiny, deep purple skin. Today, many other varieties can also be found. Long, narrow Asian eggplants have skin that is lavender or deep purple and are smaller than globe eggplants. Other types may be even smaller and have white, rose, green, or variegated skin. The color of the skin does not alter the flavor.

BELL PEPPERS BAKED WITH TOMATOES

6 bell peppers (capsicums) *(far right),* seeded and cut into strips or bite-sized pieces

12 oz (375 g) cherry tomatoes, stemmed

4–5 cloves garlic, coarsely chopped

¼ cup (2 fl oz/60 ml) extra-virgin olive oil

2 tablespoons red wine vinegar or 2 teaspoons *each* balsamic and red wine vinegar

2 teaspoons minced fresh oregano, marjoram, or thyme leaves

1 teaspoon sugar, or to taste

Salt and freshly ground pepper

2 tablespoons fresh basil leaves, torn or finely shredded

Preheat the oven to 400°F (200°C). In a large bowl, mix together the bell peppers, tomatoes, half of the garlic, the olive oil, half of the vinegar, the oregano, sugar, and salt and pepper to taste. Mix well and spread out in a single layer in a large baking pan.

Roast the vegetables for about 20 minutes. Remove from the oven, turn the vegetables so that they will brown evenly, and return them to the oven. Continue to roast until the peppers are slightly charred at the edges and the tomatoes are soft and tender and have begun to form a sauce, about 10 minutes longer.

Remove from the oven and sprinkle with the remaining garlic to taste and the remaining vinegar. Let cool until warm or room temperature. Garnish with the basil just before serving.

Serving Tips: This dish comes from Apulia, in southeast Italy, and it is as delicious at room temperature as it is warm. Serve as a side dish with roasted meats or browned sausages, toss with pasta, or pile into a crusty sandwich. It also makes a good appetizer with a mound of creamy goat cheese alongside.

MAKES 4 SERVINGS WITH LEFTOVERS

BELL PEPPER VARIETIES

Bell peppers come in a rainbow of colors. They may be used here in any combination, as long as a few red ones are included in the mix. Red bell peppers are simply the mature stage of green bell peppers, having grown considerably sweeter with the extra time spent in the sun. Sweet yellow and orange peppers pass through a green stage as well, while purple peppers are tart like their green cousins.

SUMMER SQUASH WITH SOUTHWESTERN FLAVORS

In a frying pan, heat the olive oil over medium heat. Add the squash slices and sauté until they just color lightly, about 1 minute. Then add the tomatoes, onion, garlic, chile, cumin, and sea salt to taste. Raise the heat to medium-high and cook until the squashes are tender-crisp, a few minutes longer.

Remove from the heat and stir in the lime juice. Taste and adjust the seasoning. Transfer to a serving dish, sprinkle with the cilantro, and serve at once.

MAKES 4 SERVINGS

SUMMER SQUASHES

The squashes that grow in the summer garden are thin skinned and tender, cook quickly, and are endlessly versatile. Try them sautéed, stir-fried, boiled, steamed, or broiled (grilled). Any summer squashes, or a combination, may be used in this recipe: green or golden zucchini, yellow straightneck or crookneck, bright yellow Sunburst, lime green pattypan, or striped cocozelle. Look for small- to medium-sized squashes, as large ones can be bitter and watery.

2 tablespoons extra-virgin olive oil

4 small to medium summer squashes, trimmed and cut into slices about ⅛ inch (3 mm) thick

2 medium to large ripe tomatoes, peeled (page 108) or unpeeled, chopped

1 red onion, chopped

2 cloves garlic, chopped

¼ fresh green chile, minced, or to taste

¼ teaspoon ground cumin, or to taste

Sea salt

Juice of ½ lime (1 tablespoon), or to taste

1 tablespoon chopped fresh cilantro (fresh coriander)

AUTUMN

In autumn, as the days grow shorter and a chill sets in, green market stalls overflow with vegetables that got their start under the hot summer sun. Cooks carry home snowy white heads of cauliflower, fennel bulbs with feathery tops, and hard-shelled squashes in an exotic array of colors, shapes, and sizes. The recipes that follow make the most of the season's hearty offerings.

PAN-GRILLED FENNEL AND TOMATOES

GRILL PAN

A stove-top grill pan, usually made of anodized aluminum or cast iron, is a wonderful utensil to use for grilling meats, fish, or vegetables when cold weather prevents outdoor cooking. Ridges that run across the bottom of the pan leave the characteristic grill marks that contribute flavor and a mild smokiness to the cooked foods. Grill pans of various shapes and sizes are available, including round, rectangular, or square. They are suitable for fitting over at least one or sometimes two burners.

Cut off the stems and feathery tops and any bruised outer stalks from the fennel bulbs. Slice the bulbs lengthwise ¼–½ inch (6–12 mm) thick and place in a bowl. Sprinkle the fennel with salt and toss with half of the olive oil. Set aside.

Sprinkle the cut sides of the tomatoes with the sugar, salt to taste, and the remaining olive oil.

Place a grill pan over high heat and heat it until it is very hot. Working in batches (or using 2 grill pans), place the tomatoes, round side down, on the grill pan and arrange the fennel slices alongside. (The grill pan can and should get very hot, so turn on your stove fan or open a window to take away the smoke. If the vegetables are in danger of burning, reduce the heat to medium-high.) When the tomatoes and fennel have charred on the first side, after 1–2 minutes, turn them over to char lightly on the second side. Continue cooking, moving the vegetables to the cooler parts of the pan and turning them every so often until the fennel is lightly translucent and somewhat softened and the tomatoes are heated through and lightly cooked around the edges but still firm. The total cooking time should be 5–6 minutes.

Transfer the fennel and tomatoes to a serving platter. Sprinkle with the garlic, lemon juice, and basil. Serve at once or let cool to room temperature.

Serving Tip: Make a double batch and serve the leftovers as part of an antipasto platter, or dice the cooked fennel and tomatoes and toss with thin spaghetti along with a handful of olives.

MAKES 4 SERVINGS

2 fennel bulbs, about 10 oz (315 g) each

Salt

1 tablespoon extra-virgin olive oil, or to taste

4 tomatoes, halved crosswise

Pinch of sugar

1 clove garlic, finely chopped

1 teaspoon fresh lemon juice, or to taste

10 large fresh basil leaves, finely shredded or torn (2–3 tablespoons)

CELERY ROOT PURÉED WITH TRUFFLE OIL

3 tablespoons unsalted butter

3 shallots, chopped

2 cloves garlic, chopped

1–2 celery roots (celeriacs), about 1 lb (500 g), peeled and diced *(far right)*

1 cup (8 fl oz/250 ml) chicken or vegetable stock, or as needed

½ cup (4 fl oz/125 ml) heavy (double) cream or crème fraîche (page 38)

Small pinch of freshly grated nutmeg

Salt and freshly ground pepper

1 teaspoon truffle oil, preferably black, or to taste (see Note)

In a heavy, wide sauté pan over medium heat, melt 2 tablespoons of the butter. Add the shallots and garlic and sauté lightly until softened, 1–2 minutes. Add the celery root and sauté until softened and coated with the butter, 5–7 minutes.

Pour in enough stock to cover the celery root and cook uncovered over medium heat until the celery root is just tender, about 15 minutes. The stock should be almost completely evaporated. If the celery root threatens to burn, add a little more stock; if it seems too watery at the end of the cooking, raise the heat to high for a minute or two, or long enough to evaporate all but a few tablespoons of the liquid.

Remove from the heat and let cool slightly, then transfer to a food processor and purée until smooth, adding a splash of the cream if needed. Add the rest of the cream and process to blend. Pour the purée back into the sauté pan over medium-low heat and season with the nutmeg and salt and pepper to taste. Heat through, then stir in the remaining 1 tablespoon butter.

Remove from the heat and stir in the truffle oil. Serve at once.

Note: Truffle oil is made by adding truffle shavings to olive oil, thus infusing the oil with truffle essence. White truffle oil usually comes from northern Italy, while black truffle oil comes from France. The oil is available at many gourmet food shops.

Variation Tip: Make the purée into a soup by increasing the stock to 4 cups (32 fl oz/1 l) and the cream to 2 cups (16 fl oz/500 ml).

MAKES 4 SERVINGS

TRIMMING CELERY ROOT

Celery root, also known as celeriac, is the rough and knobby root of a celery plant (though not the same one that produces the familiar celery bunches). The root's flesh has a potato-like texture and a pronounced celery flavor, and is eaten raw or cooked. To prepare it, peel away the rough skin with a paring knife. Younger roots sometimes have thinner skin, and a vegetable peeler can be used. Once the root is peeled and cut, cook it at once or toss it with lemon juice to prevent discoloration.

SHALLOTS IN RED WINE SAUCE

In a small, heavy sauté pan, melt half of the butter over low heat. When it foams, add the shallots and sauté until slightly softened and evenly coated with the butter, 6–8 minutes.

Add 2 cups (16 fl oz/500 ml) of the wine, the stock, the vinegar, the sugar, and the tarragon (if using), raise the heat to high, and bring to a boil. Reduce the heat to medium and simmer uncovered, stirring occasionally, until the shallots are cooked through and almost translucent, 10–15 minutes. The liquid should be thick and syrupy. If it cooks down too much and becomes too dark, it will be bitter, so adjust the heat if it seems to be reducing too quickly. Add the remaining ½ cup (4 fl oz/125 ml) wine and continue to simmer for a few minutes longer until reduced to a concentrated sauce; there should be ½–¾ cup (4–6 fl oz/125–180 ml) liquid.

Remove the pan from the heat and add the remaining half of the butter, stirring briskly with a fork or small whisk to incorporate the butter and give the sauce a nice gloss. Season to taste with salt and pepper and serve at once.

Serving Tip: This simple dish is an excellent accompaniment to grilled steak or salmon.

Variation Tip: Small onions such as pearl onions or tiny pickling onions, preferably red, may be used in place of the shallots.

MAKES 4 SERVINGS

PEELING SHALLOTS

You will need to peel a lot of shallots for this dish, which can be time-consuming. Here is an easy and efficient way to do it that works for small onions as well: Trim off the stem ends of each shallot. Bring a large saucepan three-fourths full of water to a boil. Add the shallots and blanch for 2 minutes. Drain, plunge into cold water, and leave in the water for 5 minutes. Drain again. The skins should slip off easily when a shallot is gently squeezed. You may need to use a paring knife to remove any stubborn skins.

3 tablespoons unsalted butter

1 lb (500 g) shallots, trimmed and peeled

2½ cups (20 fl oz/625 ml) dry red wine

1 cup (8 fl oz/250 ml) vegetable or chicken stock or low-sodium canned broth

¼ cup (2 fl oz/60 ml) balsamic vinegar

½ teaspoon sugar

1 teaspoon chopped fresh tarragon, or to taste (optional)

Salt and freshly ground pepper

AUTUMN MUSHROOM RAGOUT

2 lb (1 kg) mixed fresh mushrooms such as chanterelle, oyster, black trumpet, shiitake, cremini, and white button

2 tablespoons unsalted butter

1 red onion, finely chopped

Salt and freshly ground pepper

½ cup (4 fl oz/125 ml) dry white wine

1 cup (8 fl oz/250 ml) vegetable or chicken stock or low-sodium canned broth

½ oz (15 g) dried porcino mushrooms (cèpes), broken into small pieces

½ cup (4 fl oz/125 ml) heavy (double) cream, or as needed

Small pinch of freshly grated nutmeg

1 tablespoon chopped fresh chives or chervil

Brush the mushrooms clean *(right)* and cut them as needed so that they are roughly equal in size. In a large frying pan over medium heat, melt the butter. Add the onion and sauté until softened, about 3 minutes. Add the mushrooms, raise the heat to medium-high, and sauté until lightly browned in places, 3–5 minutes.

Season to taste with salt and pepper and add the wine. Raise the heat to high and cook until the wine is nearly evaporated, about 3 minutes. Add the stock and the dried mushrooms, reduce the heat to medium, and cook until the fresh mushrooms are tender and the dried mushrooms are rehydrated, about 10 minutes longer.

Stir in the ½ cup cream and the nutmeg, then taste and adjust the seasoning. Add more cream as desired to create a creamy but light sauce. Transfer to a warmed serving dish, sprinkle with the chives, and serve at once.

Note: See page 26 for information on mushroom varieties.

MAKES 4 SERVINGS

CLEANING MUSHROOMS

To clean mushrooms, gently brush them with a soft brush or a damp kitchen towel. It is best to avoid immersing them in water, as they are porous and soak up liquid like a sponge, which will compromise the texture and flavor of any dish. Do not brush the mushrooms too hard, or you will remove the thin outer skin that covers the caps. You only want to loosen and remove any dirt or grit. To speed the cleaning process, rinse the brush in cool water after each mushroom is cleaned.

BRUSSELS SPROUTS WITH TOASTED HAZELNUTS

Cut or pull off any dry outer leaves from the Brussels sprouts. Trim away any brown bits or spots, and slice off the dry stem end. Cut a small X about ⅛ inch (3 mm) deep into the stem end of each Brussels sprout.

Bring a large saucepan three-fourths full of water to a rolling boil. Add large pinches of salt and sugar and the trimmed Brussels sprouts and boil until the sprouts are bright green and tender, about 5 minutes. Drain, rinse under cold running water, and let drain again.

In a dry heavy frying pan over medium heat, toast the hazelnuts, stirring them to color evenly, until the skins char in places and begin to split and flake, about 10 minutes. Pour the nuts into a clean kitchen towel and roll the towel around them. Rub the nuts against one another inside the towel to remove the skins. Do not worry if some bits of skin remain. Transfer the skinned nuts to a cutting board and chop coarsely; you want an uneven mixture of some hazelnut halves and some small pieces.

Return the hazelnuts to the frying pan over medium-low heat and lightly toast the skinned nuts for 30 seconds–1 minute longer. Add the butter and let it melt. Season with salt and pepper and add the Brussels sprouts, tossing to coat them with the butter and hazelnuts and to heat through, about 5 minutes. Sprinkle with the lemon juice and serve hot or at room temperature.

MAKES 4 SERVINGS

2 lb (1 kg) Brussels sprouts

Salt and freshly ground pepper

Pinch of sugar

½ cup (2½ oz/75 g) shelled hazelnuts (filberts)

½ cup (4 oz/125 g) unsalted butter

Few drops of lemon juice

CHESTNUT VARIATION

Replace the hazelnuts with ¾ lb (375 g) chestnuts, ½ cup (4 fl oz/ 125 ml) milk, and 2 shallots, chopped. Cut an X on one side of each chestnut, drop the nuts into boiling water, and boil for 7 minutes. Drain, then peel away the hard shell and the beige inner skin. Return the nuts to the pan with the milk and add water to cover. Simmer over medium-low heat until tender, about 15 minutes. Drain. Sauté the shallots in the butter until softened, about 3 minutes. Add the chestnuts and Brussels sprouts and proceed as directed.

ROASTED SQUASH

1 orange-fleshed winter squash, such as butternut, or baking pumpkin *(far right)*, 2½ lb (1.25 kg)

3 or 4 cloves garlic, coarsely chopped

2 tablespoons extra-virgin olive oil

1 teaspoon balsamic vinegar, or to taste

½ teaspoon sugar

¼ teaspoon pure mild chile powder, preferably New Mexican, or blended chili powder

¼ teaspoon dried thyme, crumbled, or 1 teaspoon chopped fresh thyme

Salt and freshly ground pepper

Preheat the oven to 350°F (180°C). Using a large, sharp knife, cut the squash in half lengthwise through its stem end. If the skin is very hard, use a kitchen mallet to tap the knife once it is securely wedged in the squash. Scoop out the seeds and fibers and discard. Cut each squash half lengthwise again into wedges.

Arrange the squash quarters cut side up in a baking pan large enough to accommodate the pieces without touching. In a small bowl, mix together the garlic, oil, vinegar, sugar, chile powder, and thyme. Brush the mixture on the squash and season to taste with salt and pepper. Cover the pan tightly with aluminum foil.

Bake the squash until it is tender when pierced but not at all mushy, 30–40 minutes. Uncover, raise the oven temperature to 400°F (200°C), and return to the oven. Continue to roast until the squash is lightly caramelized, browned in spots, and quite tender when pierced with a fork, 10–15 minutes longer.

Transfer the squash quarters to individual serving plates and serve at once.

Variation Tip: A sprinkling of cumin in place of, or in addition to, the chile powder gives an earthy Middle Eastern flavor to this dish.

Serving Tip: Serve the squash as a hot side dish to accompany a roasted chicken or turkey, or as a room-temperature appetizer. Leftovers can be puréed and used as a filling for homemade ravioli or cannelloni.

MAKES 4 SERVINGS

WINTER SQUASHES

Winter squashes have hard shells, thick flesh, deep flavor, and dense texture as well as a long shelf life. They come in many shapes, colors, and sizes. Among the best-known orange-fleshed varieties are the beige-skinned butternut; the kabocha, with dark green skin marked with lime green stripes; the dark green, ribbed acorn; and the bumpy-skinned, gray-green or dark green Hubbard. Any of these squash varieties is suitable for this recipe. Or, use a small baking pumpkin such as the Sugar Pie, which is meaty and has a rich pumpkin flavor.

CAULIFLOWER WITH GARLIC BREAD CRUMBS

FRESH BREAD CRUMBS
You can purchase ready-made crumbs, but they are easy to make yourself and are a great way to use bread a day or two past its peak of freshness. Use a baguette or country-style bread. Trim off the crusts and cut or tear the slices into large pieces. Put in a food processor and process until the bread forms crumbs the size you want. Alternatively, to prepare the crumbs by hand, use the crust as a handle and grate the bread on the large holes of a box grater-shredder. Discard the crust.

Bring a large saucepan three-fourths full of water to a boil. Add a pinch of salt, the sugar, and the cauliflower and boil until tender, about 5 minutes. Do not overcook. Drain, rinse under running cold water, and leave to drain. Alternatively, bring water to a boil in a steamer pan, place the cauliflower florets on a steamer rack over the water, cover, and steam until tender-crisp, also about 5 minutes. Remove the cauliflower from the rack, rinse under cold running water, and let drain.

In a large frying pan over medium heat, warm 4–5 tablespoons (2–2½ fl oz/60–75 ml) of the oil. When the oil is hot, add the crumbs and toss them constantly until they are evenly toasted, browned, and crisp, about 5 minutes. Add the garlic, turn the crumbs once or twice, and remove them from the pan. Do not allow the garlic to brown; it should be cooked only enough to flavor the crumbs.

Heat the remaining 2–3 tablespoons oil in the same pan over medium heat. Add the cauliflower and mash and break it up a bit as it lightly browns in the oil and becomes slightly tender, about 5 minutes. Do not allow the cauliflower to become crisp and dark.

Add the crispy garlic crumbs to the pan and toss them with the cauliflower over medium-low heat, mashing some of the cauliflower and allowing some of it to keep its shape, about 5 minutes. Season to taste with salt and pepper and serve hot.

MAKES 4 SERVINGS

Salt and freshly ground pepper

Pinch of sugar (if boiling cauliflower)

1 large head cauliflower, about 3 lb (1.5 kg), cut into bite-sized florets

6–8 tablespoons (3–4 fl oz/ 90–125 ml) extra-virgin olive oil or vegetable oil

2 cups (4 oz/125 g) fresh bread crumbs *(far left)*

3 cloves garlic, thinly sliced or chopped

WINTER

With the arrival of winter, roots and tubers—beets, rutabagas, parsnips, Jerusalem artichokes, sweet potatoes—and sturdy greens find their way into ovens and pans on the stove top, delivering an earthy sweetness to the table. Such wintertime fare is inevitably rustic and homey, designed to warm up diners on even the coldest winter day.

BEETS WITH GOAT CHEESE AND DILL

PREPARING BEETS

The intense color of red beets, due to a pigment called betanin, colors anything the vegetable touches red—which is why beets are said to "bleed." To minimize the bleeding, do not peel or cut into beets before cooking them. (Golden beets are also delicious and will not bleed.) Roasting beets is often preferred over boiling them, as oven heat intensifies their flavor and color, whereas boiling leaches out both. Once the beets are cooked, avoid red hands and stained wood or plastic surfaces by donning kitchen gloves and protecting the cutting surface with plastic wrap or waxed paper.

If the beet greens are attached, cut them off, leaving about 1 inch (2.5 cm) of the stem intact. Place the unpeeled beets in a baking pan just large enough to hold them. Pour water into the pan to a depth of ½–1 inch (12 mm–2.5 cm). Cover the pan with aluminum foil or a lid.

Place the pan in the oven and heat the oven to 375°F (190°C). Roast the beets, adding additional water as needed to maintain the original level, until they are tender and pierced easily with a fork, about 40 minutes for small beets, 1 hour for medium beets, and 1½–2 hours for large beets.

Remove the pan from the oven and then remove the beets from the pan. Let them cool until they are easy to handle but still quite warm, about 10 minutes, then peel them, slipping off the skins, using a paring knife in spots where they stick. Cut the beets into wedges and remove the stems.

Place the warm beets in a bowl, add the shallots, and toss to combine. Sprinkle with the sugar, salt to taste, the vinegar, and the lemon juice and mix well. Add the olive oil and dill to taste and toss again.

Spoon the warm dressed beets into a serving bowl or onto individual plates. Top with dollops of goat cheese, or crumble the cheese and sprinkle it over the top. Serve still warm or at room temperature.

MAKES 4 SERVINGS

6–8 small beets, 4 medium beets, or 3 large beets, about 1¼ lb (625 g) total weight

2 shallots or ½ red onion, chopped

1 teaspoon sugar

Salt

1 tablespoon balsamic vinegar

Juice of ½ lemon

1 tablespoon extra-virgin olive oil

1–2 tablespoons chopped fresh dill

3 oz (90 g) fresh goat cheese

WINTER SALAD OF RED CABBAGE AND DRIED FRUITS

½ red cabbage, about
1 lb (500 g), cored and
shredded or thinly sliced

Salt and freshly ground
pepper

Red wine vinegar or pear,
raspberry, or cider vinegar

5 dried apricots, diced

5 dried golden figs such as
Calimyrna (Smyrna), diced

5 dried pears, diced

5 prunes, pitted and diced

1 tart, sweet, juicy apple
such as Granny Smith,
unpeeled, cored and cut
into julienne (page 10)

1–2 tablespoons canola
oil, safflower oil, or
sunflower oil

Several pinches of ground
cumin

½ teaspoon sugar, or to
taste

2–3 heaped tablespoons
walnut pieces

In a bowl, combine the cabbage and salt, pepper, and vinegar to taste and toss well. Cover and let stand for at least 2 hours at room temperature or, preferably, overnight in the refrigerator. Drain all but 1 tablespoon of the liquid.

Add the apricots, figs, pears, prunes, and apple to the cabbage and toss well. Drizzle with 1 tablespoon of the oil and add the cumin, sugar, and salt and pepper to taste. Toss well, then taste and adjust the seasoning with additional oil, vinegar, cumin, sugar, salt, and/or pepper.

Just before serving, add the walnuts and toss to mix well.

Variation Tips: Substitute 2 tablespoons golden raisins (sultanas) for the prunes. Other winter fruits, such as pears, Fuyu persimmons, or pomegranate seeds, may be used in place of the apple.

Serving Tip: Serve the salad alongside roasted or braised duck or breaded veal or pork chops.

MAKES 4 SERVINGS

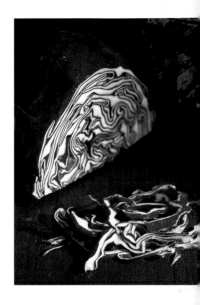

MELLOWING CABBAGE

The crunchy texture and assertive flavor of cabbage need to be tamed for some dishes. One way to do so is to blanch it for a few seconds in boiling water and then drain it promptly. Another way, as seen in this salad recipe, is to combine the cabbage with vinegar and seasonings, let it sit, and then drain it before proceeding. This will transform it from rough-textured to silky and from strong-flavored to mellow. In addition, the vinegar turns the natural blue tinge of red cabbage a bright shade of scarlet.

PUMPKIN BAKED WITH TOMATOES AND ROSEMARY

PEELING PUMPKIN

To peel a pumpkin or thick-skinned winter squash, using a sturdy chef's knife, halve the pumpkin or squash lengthwise and scoop out the seeds and fibers. Slice the halves lengthwise again into wedges. Placing each wedge skin side down on the cutting board, slice the flesh away from the peel, cutting as close to the peel as possible so that you do not lose too much of the pumpkin or squash flesh.

Peel the pumpkin *(left)*, then cut the flesh into slices ½ inch (12 mm) thick. In a heavy nonstick frying pan, heat 3 tablespoons of the olive oil over medium-high heat. In batches, lightly sauté the pumpkin slices in a single layer, turning once, until lightly browned and just tender, about 6 minutes total. Do not crowd the pan, or the slices may fall apart. Season with salt and pepper, transfer to a platter with a slotted spoon, and set aside.

Return the pan to medium heat and add the onion. Sauté lightly, adding more oil if needed to prevent scorching, until the onion is softened, about 5 minutes. Add the garlic to taste and cook until fragrant, about 1 minute, then add the tomatoes and season to taste with salt, pepper, and a pinch of sugar. Continue to cook uncovered over medium heat, stirring occasionally with a wooden spoon, until the tomatoes break down and the mixture has formed a saucelike consistency, 15–20 minutes. Stir in the rosemary and remove from the heat.

Preheat the oven to 350°F (180°C). Arrange a layer of pumpkin slices in the bottom of an 11- or 12-inch (28- or 30-cm) square or 13-by-9-inch (33-by-23-cm) rectangular baking dish with 3-inch (7.5-cm) sides. Top with about one-third of the sauce. Repeat, making 3 layers each of pumpkin and sauce and ending with a layer of sauce. Drizzle with the remaining 1 tablespoon of olive oil.

Bake until the top is lightly glazed and browned in spots and the pumpkin is tender when pierced with a knife, 35–45 minutes, checking it after about 25 minutes. Remove from the oven and serve hot or at room temperature.

MAKES 4 SERVINGS

1 baking pumpkin or winter squash (page 69), 2 lb (1 kg)

4 tablespoons (2 fl oz/ 60 ml) extra-virgin olive oil, or as needed

Salt and freshly ground pepper

1 yellow onion, chopped

3–5 cloves garlic, chopped

2 cans (12 oz/375 g each) diced tomato

Pinch of sugar

1–2 teaspoons minced fresh rosemary

BROCCOLI RABE WITH PANCETTA AND GARLIC

2 lb (1 kg) broccoli rabe, trimmed and cut into bite-sized lengths

3 oz (90 g) pancetta, diced

3 cloves garlic, chopped

2–3 tablespoons extra-virgin olive oil

Small pinch of hot red pepper flakes (optional)

Salt

Juice of ½ lemon, or to taste

Bring a large saucepan three-fourths full of water to a boil. Add the broccoli rabe and cook until just tender but still brightly colored, about 5 minutes. Drain and set aside.

In a frying pan over medium-high heat, sauté the pancetta until lightly crisp, about 5 minutes. Add the garlic, 2 tablespoons of the olive oil, and the red pepper flakes (if using), and sauté until the garlic is just slightly colored, about 1 minute. Add the broccoli rabe, adding more oil if needed to prevent scorching, and toss it with the garlic mixture until tender and heated through, 1–2 minutes longer.

Transfer the mixture to a serving dish and season to taste with salt. Add the lemon juice and toss well. Serve at once.

Variation Tips: Prepare this dish without the pancetta, let cool to room temperature, and serve as a salad. Or, toss the finished dish with freshly cooked pasta and a few dollops of ricotta cheese.

MAKES 4 SERVINGS

BROCCOLI RABE

Also known as broccoli raab, rape, and *rapini,* this relative of cabbage, turnips, and mustard shares their hearty flavor. Like broccoli, cabbage, and cauliflower, broccoli rabe is a cruciferous vegetable high in fiber, vitamins, and minerals. It has slim stalks, jagged dark green leaves, and small florets. Its pleasantly bitter flavor pairs very well with other strong flavors, as this southern Italian recipe illustrates. Be sure to remove any tough stems and wilted leaves before cooking.

JERUSALEM ARTICHOKE GRATIN

Bring a saucepan three-fourths full of salted water to a boil. Add the Jerusalem artichokes and boil until just tender when pierced with a fork, about 15 minutes. Drain and, when cool enough to handle, peel them, rubbing the skins off with your fingers or removing the skins with a paring knife. Cut into rounds ¼ inch (6 mm) thick.

Preheat the oven to 400°F (200°C). Butter an oval gratin dish about 13 inches (33 cm) long and 9 inches (23 cm) wide.

Cover the bottom of the prepared gratin dish with a layer of Jerusalem artichoke slices, overlapping them slightly. Dot with some of the butter, sprinkle with some of the garlic and parsley, and season to taste with salt and pepper. Repeat the layering until you have used up all the ingredients. Pour two-thirds of the cream evenly over the surface.

Bake until the top is crusty and the cream has become custardlike, 20–25 minutes. Remove from the oven, add the remaining cream, and return to the oven. Raise the oven temperature to 425°F (220°C) and continue to bake until the surface of the gratin is golden brown, crusty, and sizzling, about 15 minutes. Serve at once, directly from the pan.

MAKES 4 SERVINGS

2 lb (1 kg) Jerusalem artichokes

3 tablespoons unsalted butter, cut into small pieces

2 cloves garlic, chopped

2 tablespoons chopped fresh flat-leaf (Italian) parsley

Salt and freshly ground pepper

1 cup (8 fl oz/250 ml) heavy (double) cream

JERUSALEM ARTICHOKES

Despite their name, Jerusalem artichokes are neither from Jerusalem nor a relative of the artichoke. "Jerusalem" is a corruption of *girasole,* the Italian word for "sunflower." Native to North America, and also known as sunchokes, these small, pale beige tubers of the sunflower plant have a sweet, earthy, nutty flavor that is reminiscent of artichokes. If you peel or cut the tubers while they are raw, sprinkle them with lemon juice to prevent darkening. They are wonderful made into a gratin, boiled and mashed with potatoes, sautéed, or steamed.

CARROT AND CUMIN TART

1 recipe Tart Pastry
(page 111), partially blind
baked (far right)

2 tablespoons unsalted
butter

5 or 6 green (spring)
onions, white and tender
green parts, thinly sliced

Salt and freshly ground
pepper

½ teaspoon sugar

3–4 cups (12–16 oz/
375–500 g) thinly sliced,
peeled carrots

½ teaspoon cumin seeds

2 large or extra-large
whole eggs, plus 1 large
or extra-large egg yolk

1⅓ cups (11 fl oz/340 ml)
heavy (double) cream or
half-and-half (half cream)

Pinch of fresh grated
nutmeg or ground mace

1½ cups (6 oz/185 g)
shredded Gruyère,
Emmenthaler, or
Jarlsberg cheese

Prepare the deep pastry crust as directed and let it cool.

To make the filling, heat a large, heavy frying pan over medium heat until it is hot but not smoking. Add the butter. When it begins to foam, add the green onions and sauté until wilted, about 1 minute. Season with salt and pepper. Remove from the heat.

Bring a saucepan three-fourths full of water to a boil. Add salt to taste, the sugar, and the carrots and parboil until half cooked and bright orange, 1–2 minutes. Drain and set aside to cool.

In a small frying pan over medium heat, toast the cumin seeds until they are fragrant and take on a little color, 2–3 minutes. Pour onto a plate and let cool.

In a bowl, whisk together the whole eggs, egg yolk, cream, and nutmeg until blended, then season to taste with salt and pepper.

Position a rack in the upper third of the oven and preheat to 375°F (180°C). Place a baking sheet on the rack below to catch any drips.

Sprinkle half of the cheese evenly over the bottom of the cooled pastry crust. Arrange as many of the carrot slices into the crust as will fit tightly, sprinkling them with the cumin and green onions as you add them. Pour the cream mixture over the carrots, filling the tart pan almost to the rim. Sprinkle the remaining cheese over the top.

Bake until the top is golden brown and the filling is set, 25–30 minutes. Remove from the oven and let rest for at least 10 minutes. If using a tart pan with a removable bottom, place the pan on your outstretched palm and let the ring fall away, then slide the tart onto a serving plate.

MAKES 4–6 SERVINGS

BLIND BAKING

Also called prebaking, blind baking means partially or completely baking a pie or tart shell before filling it. To partially blind bake a tart shell, preheat the oven to 400°F (200°C). Lay a sheet of parchment (baking) paper over the pastry-lined tart pan; it should extend slightly beyond the rim. Weight it down with pie weights (above), raw rice, or dried beans. Bake for 10 minutes until just set, then remove the weights and parchment. Prick the bottom of the still-soft crust with a fork and return to the oven until the crust sets and colors slightly, 5–10 minutes longer. Let cool on a rack before filling.

ROASTED WINTER ROOT VEGETABLES

Preheat the oven to 425°F (220°C). Cut the sweet potatoes, parsnips, rutabagas, and carrots into large two-bite chunks (about 1½ inches/4 cm square). Peel the shallots (page 62). Leave them whole if they are small or halve them if they are large.

Place all of the vegetables in a roasting pan that is large enough to accommodate them in a single layer. Drizzle the vegetables with the olive oil and sprinkle with the garlic, the thyme, and salt and pepper to taste.

Roast the vegetables, turning them once or twice to ensure even cooking, until they are tender when pierced with a fork and browned at the edges, 35–40 minutes. Serve at once.

MAKES 4 SERVINGS

1 lb (500 g) sweet potatoes or yams, peeled

½ lb (250 g) parsnips, peeled

½ lb (250 g) rutabagas, peeled

½ lb (250 g) carrots, peeled

8–10 shallots

3 tablespoons extra-virgin olive oil

2–4 cloves garlic, coarsely chopped

1–2 teaspoons fresh thyme leaves or ¼ teaspoon dried thyme, crumbled

Salt and freshly ground pepper

RUTABAGAS

This member of the cabbage family resembles an overgrown turnip, which is often seen alongside it in the market. Rutabagas come in a variety of colors—most commonly yellow but also brown or white—and go by a variety of names, including swede, Swedish turnip, and yellow turnip. The mustardy taste of its dense yellow flesh mellows and sweetens upon cooking. Look for firm specimens free of blemishes; smaller ones are typically more tender and less pungent. After peeling, sprinkle with lemon juice to prevent the flesh from discoloring.

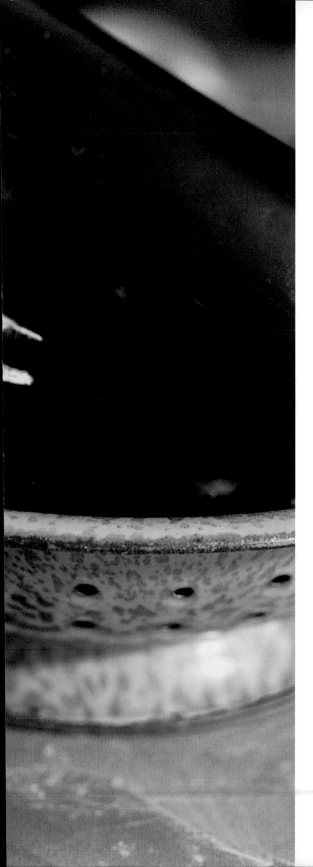

MAIN DISHES

Today, more and more cooks have access to fresher, tastier vegetables at a growing number of farmers' markets and greengrocers. And, nearly everyone is also concerned about eating more vegetables in the interest of good health. Vegetable main dishes take advantage of both these trends with delicious results. The recipes that follow draw from cuisines around the world.

BUTTERNUT SQUASH RISOTTO WITH SAGE

In a small bowl, using a fork, crush the garlic with a pinch of salt. Set aside. Halve the squash and scoop out the seeds and fibers. Peel the halves (page 78), then cut one half into ½-inch (12-mm) dice and coarsely shred the remaining half using the large holes of a grater-shredder or a food processor.

Pour the stock into a saucepan, bring to a simmer over medium heat, and adjust the heat to maintain a gentle simmer.

In a large, heavy saucepan, melt half of the butter with the olive oil over medium heat. Add the diced squash and the onion and sauté until softened, 5–7 minutes. Raise the heat to medium-high, add the rice, and cook, stirring, until the kernels are coated with the butter and oil and are opaque, 3–5 minutes.

Add the sage and pour in ¾ cup (6 fl oz/180 ml) of the wine. Cook, stirring, until the wine is absorbed. Stir in the remaining wine and again cook and stir until absorbed. Now, begin adding the hot stock about ½ cup (4 fl oz/125 ml) at a time, stirring until almost all the stock is absorbed before adding more. When the rice is almost tender, after about 15 minutes, stir in the reserved shredded squash. Continue to cook, adding more stock and stirring constantly, until the rice is firm but tender and the center of each kernel is no longer chalk-white, 20–25 minutes total. Stir in the crushed garlic, the nutmeg, and salt and pepper to taste. Add additional hot stock if necessary.

Stir in Parmesan cheese to taste, then spoon the risotto into warmed soup plates. Divide the remaining butter into 4 equal pats, and top each serving with a pat of butter and additional Parmesan if desired. Serve at once.

MAKES 4 SERVINGS

RICE FOR RISOTTO

Arborio is the best-known rice for making risotto. It is traditionally grown in the Po Valley southwest of Milan, although it is now being cultivated by some American growers as well. Among the other excellent rices for risotto are Vialone Nano and Carnaroli. All of them are high in starch, which ensures a creamy dish, and are hard, so that they cook up firm yet tender. Americans term these rices medium grain, although the Italians and others consider them short grain.

2–3 cloves garlic, chopped

Salt

1 small butternut squash, other winter squash, or pumpkin, about 1 lb (500 g)

3–4 cups (24–32 fl oz/ 750 ml–1 l) vegetable or chicken stock

About 4 tablespoons (2 oz/60 g) unsalted butter

2 tablespoons extra-virgin olive oil

1 yellow onion, chopped

1½ cups (10½ oz/330 g) Arborio rice

About 5 fresh sage leaves, finely shredded

1½ cups (12 fl oz/375 ml) dry white wine

Pinch of freshly grated nutmeg

Freshly ground pepper

¾–1 cup (3–4 oz/90–125 g) grated Parmesan cheese

RATATOUILLE

2 medium eggplants
(aubergines), about 1 lb
(500 g) total weight

2 zucchini (courgettes),
about 12 oz (375 g) total
weight

Salt and freshly ground
pepper

½ cup (4 fl oz/125 ml)
extra-virgin olive oil

2 yellow onions, thinly
sliced

1 red bell pepper (cap-
sicum), seeded and diced

1 green bell pepper (cap-
sicum), seeded and diced

5 cloves garlic, coarsely
chopped

1½ lb (750 g) fresh toma-
toes, peeled and diced
(page 108), or 2 cans
(12 oz/375 g each) diced
tomatoes, with juice

1–2 tablespoons tomato
paste (if using fresh
tomatoes)

2–3 tablespoons chopped
fresh flat-leaf (Italian)
parsley

3 fresh thyme sprigs

5–8 large fresh basil
leaves, finely shredded

Trim off the stems from the eggplants. Quarter lengthwise and then cut the quarters crosswise into slices ½ inch (12 mm) thick. Trim the zucchini and cut into slices ¼ inch (6 mm) thick. Lightly sprinkle the eggplant and zucchini pieces with salt. Let sit for about 30 minutes, then wipe with paper towels to remove excess salt.

In a frying pan, heat 2 tablespoons of the olive oil over medium-high heat. Add the onions and sauté until almost softened, about 5 minutes. Add the bell peppers and half of the garlic and cook over medium-low heat until the peppers are softened, about 7 minutes. Transfer to a heavy saucepan or Dutch oven.

Return the frying pan to medium-high heat and add 2 more table-spoons of the olive oil. Add the eggplant pieces and sauté until lightly browned on both sides, 6–7 minutes. Take care not to stir them too much or you will mash them. Add the eggplant to the onions and peppers.

Return the frying pan to medium-high heat and add 2 additional tablespoons olive oil. Add the zucchini slices and sauté until they are golden, 4–5 minutes. Add to the other vegetables.

Add the remaining garlic, the fresh tomatoes or canned tomatoes with their juice, the tomato paste (if using), and the parsley, thyme, and basil to the saucepan and stir well. Season to taste with salt and pepper. Place over medium-low heat and simmer, turning once or twice, until most of the liquid has evaporated, 20–30 min-utes. If needed, remove the vegetables from the pan with a slotted spoon and raise the heat to high, letting the liquid reduce to a saucelike consistency before recombining with the vegetables.

Remove from the heat and stir in the remaining 2 tablespoons oil. Taste and adjust the seasoning. Serve hot or at room temperature.

MAKES 4 SERVINGS

RATATOUILLE

One of the great dishes of Provençal cuisine, ratatouille is a delicious mélange of vegetables, herbs, and garlic from the summer garden. Like many rustic dishes, it tastes best the day after it is cooked, when the flavors have had a chance to meld. Serve it hot with roasted or grilled lamb, chicken, or pork, or try it cold as a refreshing antidote to the season's hottest days.

SPANISH OMELET
OF POTATO, PEPPER, AND TOMATO

Heat a large, heavy ovenproof frying pan over medium heat. Add 3 tablespoons of the oil, the potatoes, onion, rosemary, and half of the garlic to taste. Stir well, reduce the heat to low, season with salt and pepper, cover, and cook, turning the potatoes once or twice, until the potatoes are just cooked through, about 15 minutes.

Transfer the potatoes to a bowl and return the pan to medium-high heat. Add 2 tablespoons of the oil. When hot, add the peppers and sauté until soft, about 7 minutes. Add the tomatoes and cook until they break down into a thick sauce, 7–10 minutes. Season with salt and pepper, add the remaining garlic to taste and the basil, and mix well. Transfer to a bowl separate from the potatoes.

In a small bowl, beat 5 of the eggs until blended and add to the potatoes. Beat the remaining eggs and add to the tomato mixture.

Preheat the broiler (grill). Wipe the frying pan clean, return it to medium-high heat, and add the remaining 3 tablespoons olive oil. When the oil is hot, pour in the potato mixture and cook without disturbing for about 2 minutes. Reduce the heat to medium-low and continue to cook, using a spatula to lift the edges of the omelet every so often to allow the liquid egg to flow beneath the potato mixture. When the eggs are almost firm, after about 7 minutes, pour in the tomato mixture and spread it in an even layer. Reduce the heat to very low, cover, and cook, checking the omelet occasionally to make sure the bottom is not sticking, until the mixture has set, about 7 more minutes.

Uncover and slide the pan under the broiler and cook until the top is lightly browned, 3–4 minutes. Insert a cake tester or skewer at the center of the omelet; it should come out clean. Slide the omelet onto a serving plate. Serve hot or at room temperature.

MAKES 4 SERVINGS

SPANISH OMELET

A Spanish omelet, known as a *tortilla española,* is a classic element of the Iberian table, eaten as a tapa, for lunch, or as a light supper. The featured ingredient, whether vegetable, meat, or fish, is first sautéed and then bound together with beaten egg and cooked into a flat cake in a pan on the stove top. Typically, Spanish cooks flip the *tortilla* in the pan to brown the second side— a maneuver that requires some practice—but the recipe has been simplified here by sliding the omelet under the broiler to cook the top side.

½ cup (4 fl oz/125 ml) extra-virgin olive oil, or as needed

1½ lb (750 g) waxy potatoes such as Yukon gold, peeled and cut into ½-inch (12-mm) dice

1 medium-large yellow onion, chopped

1–2 teaspoons chopped fresh rosemary

5–8 cloves garlic, chopped

Salt and freshly ground pepper

2 red bell peppers (capsicums), seeded and diced

4 tomatoes, peeled (page 108), seeded, and diced

3–4 tablespoons fresh basil leaves

8 eggs

EGGPLANT AND CHICKPEA STEW
WITH TOMATOES

2 small to medium eggplants (aubergines), about 1½–2 lb (750 g–1 kg) total weight

4–5 tablespoons (2–2½ fl oz/60–75 ml) extra-virgin olive oil

1 red onion, cut into wedges

3–4 cloves garlic, coarsely chopped

1 lb (500 g) fresh tomatoes, puréed with a grater-shredder (far right)

1½ cups (9 oz/280 g) canned chickpeas (garbanzo beans)

1 lb (500 g) canned diced tomatoes, with juice

Salt and freshly ground pepper

¼ teaspoon sugar

⅛ teaspoon dried thyme, crushed

Pinch of ground cinnamon

½ cup (4 fl oz/125 ml) dry red wine

2 tablespoons chopped fresh flat-leaf (Italian) parsley

Juice of ½ lemon

Cut the eggplant crosswise into slices about ½ inch (12 mm) thick.

Heat a large, heavy frying pan over medium-high heat. When it is hot, add 2 tablespoons of the olive oil, then add the eggplant slices and fry until they are browned on the first side, about 5 minutes. Turn and brown the second side, adding 1–2 tablespoons more olive oil to the pan as needed. Remove the eggplant from the pan and set it aside.

Heat 1 tablespoon olive oil over medium heat. Sauté the onion with the garlic until the onion is softened, 5–6 minutes, then add the puréed fresh tomatoes, chickpeas, canned tomatoes with their juice, salt and pepper to taste, sugar, thyme, cinnamon, red wine, and parsley. Cook gently until the sauce is thickened and savory, about 10 minutes, stirring occasionally but taking care not to break up the chickpeas.

Add the eggplant, taking care not to break up the slices, cover, and reduce the heat to medium-low. Let simmer to marry the flavors, 10–15 minutes. Add a squeeze of lemon juice, taste for seasoning, and serve hot or at room temperature.

Serving Tip: Serve this stew with crusty French bread and a feta cheese salad, or spoon over boiled pasta or a simple rice pilaf.

MAKES 4 SERVINGS

QUICK TOMATO PURÉE
Puréeing fresh tomatoes with a grater-shredder is a simple way to add tomato flavor without having to blanch, peel, and purée tomatoes in a food processor. Working with 1 tomato at a time, cut a thin slice off the stem end and squeeze out the seeds. Grate the cut edge of the tomato on the large rasps of a handheld grater, rendering the flesh into a soft purée. Only the skin will remain, which can then be discarded.

ARTICHOKES STUFFED WITH BULGUR AND ROASTED TOMATOES

BULGUR

Nutty-tasting bulgur, also known as bulghur or burghul, was a favorite food of ancient Persians. It is made by steaming wheat, partly removing the bran, and then drying and cracking the grains. Today, it is most commonly found in Middle Eastern and Balkan cooking, where it is traditionally used as the basis for pilafs, salads, and stuffings. Sold in fine, medium, and coarse grinds, it has a mild flavor and firm texture that make it a good vehicle for the flavors of other ingredients.

Bring a large saucepan of water to a boil, add the artichokes, and boil until half cooked, about 20 minutes. Drain and let cool. In another saucepan, combine the bulgur with 2 cups (16 fl oz/500 ml) water. Place over medium-high heat and bring to a boil. Reduce the heat to low and simmer until the bulgur is almost tender, about 10 minutes.

Meanwhile, grate 5 or 6 of the tomatoes into a purée (page 97) and cut the remainder into wedges. Chop 2 of the garlic cloves, cut 4–6 cloves into slivers, and leave the remainder whole.

Add the grated tomatoes, the chopped garlic, and the mint to the bulgur and season with salt and pepper. Continue to cook until the bulgur is tender and has absorbed almost all of the liquid, a few minutes longer. Mix in 2 tablespoons of the olive oil, the parsley, and the juice from 1 lemon half and remove from the heat.

Preheat the oven to 450°F (230°C). Gently spread the leaves of each artichoke and scoop out the fuzzy choke. Fill each artichoke with one-fourth of the bulgur mixture, packing it well and mounding the top. Using about 1 garlic clove for each artichoke, slip garlic slivers between as many leaves as possible. Arrange the artichokes in a baking pan with several inches of space in between. Fill these spaces with the tomato wedges and whole garlic cloves. Drizzle the remaining oil over all, including between the leaves. Sprinkle with the juice of the other lemon half and coarse salt.

Roast until browned in spots, about 30 minutes. Reduce the heat to 325°F (165°C) and roast until the artichokes are evenly browned and the tomatoes have collapsed and darkened, about 30 minutes. Serve each artichoke with some of the roasted tomatoes and a lemon wedge alongside, spooning the juices from the pan on top.

MAKES 4 SERVINGS

4 large artichokes, stems and thorns trimmed, tough outer leaves removed (page 34)

1 cup (6 oz/185 g) medium-grind bulgur

3 lb (1.5 kg) large, ripe tomatoes

10–12 cloves garlic

3 teaspoons chopped fresh mint or 1½ teaspoons dried mint, crumbled

Coarse sea salt and freshly ground pepper

4 tablespoons (2 fl oz/60 ml) olive oil, or as needed

3–4 tablespoons chopped fresh flat-leaf (Italian) parsley

2 lemons, 1 halved and 1 cut into wedges

VEGETABLE STIR-FRY WITH TOFU

2–4 cloves garlic

1 small to medium carrot

1 red bell pepper (capsicum)

1 yellow onion

1 white cabbage, about
1½ lb (750 g)

¾ lb (375 g) firm tofu,
drained

Cornstarch (cornflour) for
dusting

3 tablespoons canola oil

1 tablespoon peeled and
chopped fresh ginger

Salt

¼–½ teaspoon Chinese
five-spice powder

3–4 tablespoons (1½–2 fl oz/
45–60 ml) chicken stock

1 tablespoon sugar

3–4 tablespoons (1½–2 fl oz/
45–60 ml) hoisin sauce

Few dashes of soy sauce

Few dashes of chili oil

Few dashes of rice vinegar

½ teaspoon sesame oil

1½ cups (10½ oz/330 g)
white rice, cooked according
to package directions

Chop the garlic. Peel and slice the carrot on the diagonal. Seed the bell pepper and cut into large dice. Slice the onion lengthwise. Core the cabbage and cut into large dice. Cut the tofu into 1-inch (2.5-cm) cubes, blot dry with paper towels, dust the cubes with the cornstarch, and blot again with paper towels.

In a wok or deep frying pan, preferably nonstick, heat 1 table-spoon of the oil over medium-high heat, swirling it to coat the pan. Add the tofu and cook until lightly browned on the first side, 2½–4 minutes. Turn the tofu cubes over, being careful not to break them up, and continue cooking until browned on the opposite side, 2½–4 minutes longer. Transfer to a plate and set aside.

Wipe the pan clean, return it to high heat, and add 1 tablespoon of the oil, again swirling. When it is hot, add the garlic, ginger, carrot, and bell pepper and stir-fry for 1 minute. Add to the tofu.

Return the empty pan to high heat and heat the remaining 1 tablespoon oil. Add the onion and stir-fry for 1 minute. Add the cabbage and a pinch of salt and stir and toss to coat with the oil. Mix in the five-spice powder and 3 tablespoons stock and stir-fry until the cabbage has begun to soften, 5–6 minutes. Add the sugar, hoisin, soy sauce, and chili oil and stir. Add another tablespoon stock if the mixture seems dry. Cover and cook over high heat until the cabbage is almost tender-crisp, about 5 minutes.

Uncover and add the carrot mixture and tofu. Stir to blend and heat through, about 3 minutes. The liquid should be almost fully evaporated. Season with the vinegar to balance the flavors.

Mound the vegetables onto a platter and sprinkle with the sesame oil. Serve at once with the hot rice.

MAKES 4 SERVINGS

STIR-FRY SAVVY

The secret to a successful vegetable stir-fry is to cook the ingredients quickly in hot oil over high heat so that they remain crisp and crunchy. Bell peppers (capsicums), carrots, and cabbage are good sturdy vegetables for the beginning stir-fry cook. They are more forgiving than such delicate vegetables as snow peas (mangetouts) or bean sprouts, which can easily overcook. Because speed is of the essence, have all the ingredients cut, measured, and at hand next to the stove before you begin cooking.

LEEK AND GOAT CHEESE TART

Prepare the deep pastry crust as directed and let it cool.

In a large, heavy frying pan, melt the butter over medium-low heat. When it foams, add the leeks, reduce the heat to low, and cook slowly until the leeks are soft and golden, about 15 minutes. Season with salt and pepper and set aside to cool.

Position a rack in the upper third of the oven and preheat the oven to 350°F (180°C). Place a baking sheet on the rack below to catch any drips.

In a bowl, whisk together the whole eggs, egg yolk, and cream until blended. Season with the nutmeg, salt, and pepper.

Sprinkle half of the shredded cheese evenly over the bottom of the pastry crust. Top with the leeks, then the chives, and finally the goat cheese. Pour in as much of the egg mixture as will fit, stopping within ½ inch (12 mm) of the rim. Sprinkle the remaining shredded cheese evenly over the top.

Bake the tart until the top is lightly puffed and golden and the filling jiggles only slightly when the pan is gently shaken, about 25 minutes. Remove the tart from the oven and let rest for at least 10 minutes. If using a tart pan with a removable bottom, place the pan on your outstretched palm and let the ring fall away, then slide the tart onto a serving plate. Serve hot or at room temperature.

MAKES 4–6 SERVINGS

CLEANING LEEKS

Leeks are grown in sandy soil, so they need to be cleaned carefully to rid them of the grit that hides in among the long, leafy fronds. Using a sharp knife, trim off the roots and the tough green tops. Peel away the outer layer, which is often wilted or discolored. Cut a slit lengthwise down the middle of the leek, extending it about three-fourths of the way through the heart of the leek and stopping where the white changes to green. Rinse the slit leek well under cold running water, gently pulling apart the leaf layers to rinse away all of the grit.

1 recipe Tart Pastry (page 111), partially blind baked (page 85)

2 tablespoons unsalted butter

1 lb (500 g) leeks, including tender green parts, well cleaned (far left) and sliced crosswise ⅛ inch (3 mm) thick

Salt and freshly ground pepper

2 whole eggs, plus 1 egg yolk

1 cup (8 fl oz/250 ml) heavy (double) cream or half-and-half (half cream)

Pinch of freshly grated nutmeg

1 cup (4 oz/125 g) shredded Gruyère, Emmenthaler, or Jarlsberg cheese

3 tablespoons chopped fresh chives

¼ lb (125 g) fresh goat cheese, crumbled

VEGETABLE BASICS

The designation "vegetable side dish" once meant a second thought—the element that turned meat and potatoes into a meal. Today this is no longer true. The plain boiled vegetables of the past have given way to a whole new philosophy of cooking that puts fresh vegetables in a more prominent place on the table, adding color, flavor, and appeal to any meal.

THE SEASONAL APPROACH

The first key to delicious vegetable dishes is to follow the seasons. Any vegetable that has been locally grown and ripened in its natural season will be infinitely more flavorful than a semiripe specimen transported from the other side of the country or the other side of the globe. Visit a local farmers' market to find the freshest vegetables of the season, and you can't help but feel inspired in the kitchen. Or, if you have a green thumb and a bit of space, you can do the growing yourself. Nothing is more flavorful than vegetables dug up from your own garden just minutes before cooking.

Following is a list of vegetables to look for at different times during the year. Bear in mind that vegetables don't watch the calendar, however, and that their availability will vary with location and weather.

SPRING

Shoots and Stalks: Artichokes and asparagus.

Leaves: Arugula (rocket), baby spinach, kale, lettuces, and mâche.

Cabbage Family: Broccoli rabe and cabbage.

Roots and Tubers: Daikon, new potatoes, radishes, turnips, and young ginger.

Mushrooms: Buttons, morels, oysters, porcini, portobellos, and shiitakes.

Peas, Beans, and Seeds: English peas, fava (broad) beans, and green beans.

Bulbs: Baby leeks, green garlic, green (spring) onions, and Vidalia onions.

SUMMER

Leaves: Arugula, romaine (cos) lettuce, and spinach.

Vegetable Fruits: Bell peppers (capsicums), chiles, eggplants (aubergines), summer squashes, tomatillos, tomatoes, and zucchini (courgettes).

Roots and Tubers: Carrots, ginger, and potatoes.

Peas, Beans, and Seeds: Corn, English peas, green beans, haricots verts, wax beans, and shelling beans such as cranberry or flageolet.

Bulbs: Garlic, leeks, onions, and shallots.

AUTUMN

Shoots and Stalks: Artichokes and fennel.

Leaves: Spinach and Swiss chard.

Cabbage Family: Broccoli, broccoli rabe, Brussels sprouts, cabbage, and cauliflower.

Vegetable Fruits: Bell peppers, eggplants, pumpkins, and winter squashes.

Roots and Tubers: Celery root (celeriac), parsnips, potatoes, rutabagas, sweet potatoes, turnips, and yams.

Mushrooms: Black trumpets, buttons, chanterelles, oysters, porcini, portobellos, and shiitakes.

Bulbs: Garlic, leeks, and shallots.

WINTER

Leaves: Frisée, kale, radicchio, Swiss chard, and turnip greens.

Cabbage Family: Broccoli, broccoli rabe, Brussels sprouts, and cabbage.

Roots and Tubers: Beets, carrots, celery root, Jerusalem artichokes, parsnips, rutabagas, sweet potatoes, turnips, and yams.

Mushrooms: Buttons, chanterelles, portobellos, and truffles.

CHOOSING & STORING

When choosing vegetables, look for the freshest ones you can find. As they sit in the market, they will lose moisture and vitamins and their flavor begins to dissipate. Fresh vegetables should look plump, moist, and unwrinkled. At a farmers' market, you can ask the farmer when the vegetables were picked. Often, you'll be offered a sample to taste.

Some vegetables, such as corn on the cob, tomatoes, and artichokes, begin to lose their freshness as soon as they are harvested. Others, such as hard-shelled winter squashes, potatoes, and carrots, can be stored for relatively long periods of time.

Tender leafy greens do not keep well; store them in the vegetable crisper of your refrigerator for only a few days. When their leaf edges turn brown or the leaves show signs of decay, discard them.

Cabbage and root vegetables such as turnips are good keepers. These wintertime vegetables can hold onto their flavor, texture, and nutrients for several weeks after harvesting. Store them in the vegetable crisper of the refrigerator for up to 2 weeks. Sturdy summer vegetables, such as zucchini and eggplant, also do well in the crisper, but for a shorter time.

Onions, shallots, and garlic can all be stored at room temperature and will usually last about 3 weeks. Keep them in a cool place, preferably in a basket where the air can circulate. Potatoes must be stored in the dark, as light will cause them to turn green and bitter.

PREPARING VEGETABLES

Most vegetables need to be cleaned as their first preparation step. Wash them under cold running water, then set them out to dry before using. If you are in a hurry, use paper towels or a clean kitchen towel to dry them. Mushrooms, which are porous and soak up water, should not be rinsed. Use a soft brush or a damp cloth to wipe them clean. Peas and fresh shell beans just need to be popped from their pods. Onion, garlic, and shallots require only peeling.

BASIC TECHNIQUES

Chopping coarsely: To chop long, thin vegetables such as celery coarsely, first slice them lengthwise into halves or quarters, then hold the pieces together and cut crosswise.

To coarsely chop an onion or other round vegetable, see the basic steps shown opposite:

1 **Cut the onion in half:** Slice the stem end off of the onion, halve it lengthwise from the stem to root end, then peel it.

2 **Make a series of vertical cuts:** Put an onion half flat side down on a cutting board, holding it with your fingertips safely curled under and away from the blade, and, with the knife tip pointed toward the root end, make a series of parallel vertical cuts at right angles to the cutting board. Do not cut all the way through the root end.

3 **Make a series of horizontal cuts:** Turn the knife so that it is parallel with the cutting board and perpendicular to the first series of cuts, and make a series of horizontal cuts in the onion half, again not cutting through the root end.

4 **Chop the onion:** Simply slice the onion across the 2 cuts made in steps 2 and 3.

Chopping finely: For a finer chop, gather coarsely chopped vegetables into a pile. Chop the vegetables to the desired fineness, holding the knife tip down on the cutting board with one hand while rocking the blade up and down across the pile as you chop.

Coring: A tough core, sometimes found in celery root or fennel, is unpleasant to eat and should be removed. To do this, cut the vegetable

GLOSSARY

ALMONDS Delicately flavored almonds are excellent when added to many vegetable dishes. To blanch, or peel, almonds, place the shelled nuts in a heatproof bowl and pour boiling water over them. Let stand for about 1 minute, then drain in a colander and rinse with cold running water to cool. Pinch each nut to slip off its bitter skin.

BASIL Used in kitchens throughout the Mediterranean and in Southeast Asia, basil tastes faintly of anise and cloves. Many different varieties are available, including common green Italian basil and reddish purple Thai basil.

BUTTER, UNSALTED Many cooks favor unsalted butter for two reasons. First, salt in butter can add to the total amount of salt in a recipe, which can interfere with the taste of the final dish. Second, unsalted butter is likely to be fresher, since salt acts as a preservative and prolongs shelf life. If you cannot find unsalted butter, salted butter will work in most recipes, but taste and adjust other salt in the recipe as needed.

CAYENNE PEPPER A very hot ground red pepper made from dried cayenne and other chiles, cayenne can be used sparingly in a wide variety of recipes to add heat or heighten flavor. Always begin with a small amount and add more to taste in tiny increments.

CHERVIL This springtime herb has feathery leaves and a taste reminiscent of parsley and anise. It is a nice addition to vegetables, salads, and soups.

CHILES, HANDLING To reduce the heat of a chile, cut out the membranes, or ribs, and discard the seeds. This is where the capsaicin, the compound that gives a chile its heat, is concentrated. If you like heat, leave in a few seeds. Avoid touching your eyes, nose, and mouth while you are working with chiles. When finished, thoroughly wash your hands, the cutting board, and the knife with hot, soapy water. Wear kitchen gloves when working with especially hot chiles to prevent burns to your fingers.

CHILE POWDER VS. CHILI POWDER Pure chile powder is the lightly toasted ground powder of an individual variety of chile, such as New Mexican or pasilla. Chili powder is a commercial spice blend that combines ground dried chiles with spices such as cumin, garlic, oregano, and coriander.

DUTCH OVEN These large, heavy round or oval pots with tight-fitting lids and two loop handles are used for slow cooking on the stove top or in the oven. Most are made of enameled cast iron, although some are made of uncoated cast iron or other metals. They are also called casseroles and stew pots.

EGG, RAW Eggs are sometimes used raw or partially cooked in sauces and other preparations. These eggs run a risk of being infected with salmonella or other bacteria, which can lead to food poisoning. This risk is of most concern to small children, older people, pregnant women, and anyone with a compromised immune system. If you have health and safety concerns, do not consume under-cooked egg, or seek out a pasteurized egg product to replace it. Eggs can also be made safe by heating them to a temperature of 140°F (60°C) for 3½ minutes. Note that coddled, poached, and soft-boiled eggs are often undercooked.

EGGS, SEPARATING When separating egg whites from egg yolks, start with cold eggs, which separate more easily than room-temperature eggs. Position 3 bowls side by side. Carefully crack each egg sharply on its equator on a flat surface and, holding it over a bowl, pass the yolk back and forth between the shell halves and let the whites run into the bowl. Drop the yolk into the second bowl, and transfer the whites to the third bowl. Separate each additional egg over an empty bowl, for if any speck of yolk gets into the whites, the whites will not whip up properly. If a yolk breaks, start fresh with a new egg. You can also pour the yolk and whites into your clean, cupped hand, letting the whites run through your fingers into one of the bowls and depositing the yolk in another. Or, use an egg separator, a small bowl-shaped device with a depression made to hold the yolk while the white slips through. Let the separated eggs come to room temperature before using.

FENNEL Similar in appearance to celery, but with a large bulb on the end from which slimmer stems emerge, fennel has a faint licorice flavor and a crisp texture. It is available year-round but is at its peak from October to March. Select creamy-colored bulbs topped by fresh-looking stems and feathery green tops. If a recipe calls only for the bulb, cut off the stems and trim away the base of the core if it is thick and discolored.

FOOD MILL Used to purée cooked or soft foods, this tool looks like a saucepan with a perforated bottom and an interior crank-shaped handle. A paddle-shaped blade at the base rotates against a disk perforated with small holes. As the handle is turned, the blade forces the food through the holes. Some mills have interchangeable disks with variously sized holes, while others have a fixed disk.

FRYING PAN This broad pan is often confused with a sauté pan, but differs in that its flared sides make it useful for cooking foods that must be stirred or turned out of the pan. Keep small and large frying pans on hand.

GARLIC Each bulb, or head, of garlic is a cluster of 12 to 16 cloves, individually covered and collectively wrapped with papery white to purplish red skin that must be peeled before eating. Choose plump heads with smooth, firm cloves and no green sprouts.

GINGER Fresh ginger is a knobby-looking rhizome with smooth, golden skin. Peel first and then cut or grate as directed in individual recipes. Do not substitute ground dried ginger for fresh.

HAZELNUTS Also known as filberts, grape-sized hazelnuts have hard shells that come to a point like an acorn, cream-colored flesh, and a sweet, rich, buttery flavor. Difficult to crack, they are usually sold already shelled. See page 66.

LEMONS To juice a lemon, roll it firmly against a hard, flat surface or between your palms to crush some of its inner membrane. Slice the lemon in half cross-wise and use a reamer with ridged edges to extract the juice. A fork inserted into the cut surface of the lemon and rotated back and forth will work almost as well.

For zest, choose an organic lemon if possible and scrub it well to remove any wax or residue. Use a zester (a tool that removes the zest in thin strips), a paring knife, or a vegetable peeler to cut off only the thin, colored portion of the rind, taking care not to include the bitter white pith. To grate the zest, remove it with the fine rasps of a handheld grater.

MANDOLINE A flat, rectangular tool ideal for cutting food quickly and easily. A mandoline usually comes with an assortment of smooth and corrugated blades, so food can be sliced, julienned, or waffle-cut. Food is moved over the very sharp blades with a strumming motion, which gives the tool its name. Metal French mandolines and plastic Asian slicers are available. If your model does not have a hand guard, keep your hand as flat as possible and your fingers away from the blades when slicing.

NUTMEG The brown, oblong seed of a tropical evergreen tree. When first removed from the fruit, the nutmeg is enclosed in a lacy red covering that, when lifted away and ground, is known as the spice mace. Always purchase whole nutmegs and grate them on a specialized nutmeg grater or the fine rasps of a handheld grater just before use.

OILS
Canola: This bland oil is pressed from rapeseed, a relative of the mustard plant, High in monounsaturated fat, it is good for general cooking.

Olive: Extra-virgin olive oil, made from olives pressed without the use of heat, has a fresh, full-bodied flavor and green color that ranges from quite dark to pale. Extra-virgin olive oil is generally used in uncooked preparations. Regular olive oil (formerly called pure, but now sold without any particular designation) is extracted through the use of heat. Golden in color, it is less flavorful than extra-virgin and is good for sautéing.

Peanut: Pressed from peanuts, this oil has a hint of rich, nutty flavor, unless it is a refined version. It is popular in Asian cooking for stir-frying or deep-frying.

OLIVES

Kalamata: A popular olive variety from Greece, the Kalamata is almond shaped, purplish black, rich, and meaty. The olives are brine cured and then packed in oil or vinegar.

Niçoise: A small, brownish black olive from Provence, the Niçoise is brine cured and packed in oil with lemon and herbs.

ONIONS

Green: Also known as scallions or spring onions, green onions are the immature shoots of the bulb onion, with a narrow white base that has not yet begun to swell and long, flat green leaves. They are mild in flavor and can be enjoyed raw, stir-fried, grilled, braised, or chopped as a garnish.

Pearl: Pearl onions are small onions no more than 1 inch (2.5 cm) in diameter. They are traditionally white, although red ones are now available.

Red: Also called Bermuda onions or Italian onions, red onions are purplish and slightly sweet. They are delicious raw and briefly cooked in vegetable mixes.

Shallot: A small member of the onion family that looks like a large clove of garlic covered with papery bronze or reddish skin, a shallot has white flesh lightly streaked with purple, a crisp texture, and a subtle flavor.

Yellow: The yellow globe onion is the common, all-purpose onion sold in supermarkets. It can be globular, flattened, or slightly elongated, and has parchmentlike golden brown skin. Usually too harsh for serving raw, it becomes rich and sweet when cooked, making it ideal for caramelizing.

PANCETTA Unsmoked Italian bacon made by rubbing a slab of pork belly with spices that may include pepper, cinnamon, cloves, or juniper berries, then rolling the slab into a tight cylinder and curing it for at least 2 months.

PARMESAN CHEESE Look for the authentic Italian version of this firm grating cheese, made in Emilia-Romagna, as its flavor and texture are far superior to those of its many imitators. True Parmesan cheese will have the words Parmigiano-Reggiano stamped in a pattern on the rind. Always use freshly grated Parmesan for the best flavor.

PARSLEY Two types of parsley are commonly available: curly-leaf parsley and flat-leaf, or Italian, parsley. The latter has a more pronounced flavor and is preferred for recipes in this book.

PARSNIP A relative of the carrot, this ivory-colored root closely resembles its brighter, more familiar cousin. Parsnips have a slightly sweet flavor and a tough, starchy texture that softens with cooking. They are excellent roasted, steamed, boiled, or baked.

POTATOES

Russet: Also called baking or Idaho potatoes, these large, oval tubers have dry, reddish brown skin and a starchy flesh that is perfect for baking.

Yukon gold: All-purpose potatoes with thin yellowish skins and golden, fine-grained, buttery-tasting flesh. They hold their shape well when boiled, and thus may be used in the same ways as red and white boiling potatoes and new potatoes. They are also good roasted.

POTATO RICER A ricer is composed of a small pot with a perforated bottom and a plunger attached to the rim. The plunger forces the potatoes or other softly cooked root vegetables through the holes. The result is soft ricelike kernels of vegetable, which, when stirred, produce a very fine mash.

ROQUEFORT This sheep's milk cheese from France is aged in limestone caves near the village of Roquefort-sur-Soulzon in the Midi-Pyrénées. Roquefort has a moist, crumbly interior and a true, clean, strong flavor.

SAUTÉ PAN Straight-sided pan with a high, angled handle, relatively high sides so that the food can be easily flipped without fear of spilling, and usually a lid. Sauté pans are also useful for braised dishes or any stove-top recipe that calls for a lot of liquid.

STEAMER BASKET See Steaming, page 110.

INDEX

APPLE PRESS
Sheridan House, 4th Floor
112-116A Western Road
Hove , East Sussex BN3 1DD
United Kingdom

WELDON OWEN INC.
Chief Executive Officer: John Owen
President: Terry Newell
Chief Operating Officer: Larry Partington
Vice President, International Sales: Stuart Laurence
Creative Director: Gaye Allen
Series Editor: Sarah Putman Clegg
Associate Editor: Heather Belt
Production Manager: Chris Hemesath
Production Assistant: Donita Boles
Studio Manager: Brynn Breuner
Photograph Editor: Lisa Lee

A Weldon Owen Production
Copyright © 2002 by Weldon Owen Inc. and
Williams-Sonoma Inc.

First Apple Press edition printed in 2003.

ISBN 1 84092 415 2

10 9 8 7 6 5 4 3 2 1

Set in Trajan, Utopia, and Vectora.

Color separations by Bright Arts Graphics
Singapore (Pte.) Ltd.
Printed and bound in Singapore by Tien Wah
Press (Pte.) Ltd.

A NOTE ON WEIGHTS AND MEASURES

All recipes include customary U.S. and metric measurements. Metric conversions are based on
a standard developed for these books and have been rounded off. Actual weights may vary.